MAKING SENSE OF PLACE:

New approaches to place marketing

Chris Murray

The author

Chris Murray is currently Cultural Planning Manager for Milton Keynes Council. He has studied and practised marketing in different environments and holds the Diploma in Marketing from the Chartered Institute of Marketing. This publication is based on research undertaken whilst studying for the MA in European Cultural Planning with De Montfort University Leicester.

With thanks to: Charles Landry, Director, COMEDIA, for support, guidance and editing; to Dr. Franco Bianchini, Director, International Cultural Planning and Policy Unit, De Montfort University Leicester, for supervision of the initial research project and thesis; to Jonathan Hyams for additional material and editing; to John Lewis, Project Director, English Partnerships; and to Dr. Nick Jewson, Visual Sociology Group, Leicester University.

First published in the UK 2001 by Comedia, in association with the Cultural Planning and Research Unit, De Montfort University Leicester.

A catalogue record for this book is available from the British Library

ISBN 1 873667 18 3

Comedia,
The Round, Bournes Green
Near Stroud, GL6 7NL, UK
http://www.comedia.org

International Cultural Planning and Policy Unit
Department of Media and Cultural Production
Faculty of Humanities
De Montfort University
Clephan Building
The Gateway
Leicester LE1 9BH
0116 2577391

Cover design, Sue Murray
Typesetting, IDILIK CREATIVE
Printed and bound by Da Costa Print/The Book Factory, Pims House, Mildmay Avenue, London N1 4RS

This and other Comedia publications available through:
Eco-Distribution
Croswell, Eglywswrw
Pembrokeshire, SA41 3TE
0123 989 1431
jill.chandler@virgin.net

Contents

3. Foreword: Dr. Franco Bianchini

5. The landscape of place marketing

6. Mapping the territory
9. The research summarised
12. New vistas - shifting the perspective
14. Appointing Local Ambassadors
16. Redrawing the map -the six step approach outlined

19. Exploring place marketing – the research project

20. Analysis and interpretation
22. Defining the landscape - the research results
27. Measuring the contours - the research scores
28. Framing the view - what do the results mean?

42. From images to icons

43. Taking in the view
45. Symbols and signs
46. Beacon concepts

48. Scoping the problem

49. From brochures to visits
52. From products to places
54. I don't recognise my city!
60. The right tools for the job?

63. Place, identity and self

64. Identity as a commodity
70. Digging at the roots – identity uncovered
74. Identity in the regions
75. The Value of identity

80. Defining the solution

81. Globally competitive cities
84. Three fundamental problems
86. An alternative, Cultural Planning approach

89. **The future of place marketing practice: six Key Actions**

90. 1. Integration
91. 2. Participate to innovate
93. 3. From place marketing to place development
98. 4. The right tools for the job: a new place marketer's toolkit
102. The Place Development Matrix
109. 5. Breaking the mould - retraining the professionals
111. 6. Shifting the mind-set: a new definition of place

112. **Summary and conclusions**

113. Seven central issues

117. **Bibliography**

120. **Recent Comedia publications**

Foreward

Dr. Franco Bianchini

**Director,
International Cultural
Planning and Policy Unit
De Montfort University
Leicester**

Making Sense of Place is built on research Chris conducted for his final dissertation for the MA in European Cultural Planning at our University (gained, with Distinction, in February 2000). I was Chris's Supervisor and realised that he possesses a rare combination of skills and knowledge, enabling him to produce this important critique of place marketing practice. He has a strong grasp of marketing and is professionally qualified, but is also a trained art theorist and practitioner, a local government cultural planner, and is familiar with crucial debates in psychology, having worked in arts and psychiatry in London in the late 80's.

Chris's book advocates the importance of an interdisciplinary and creative approach to understanding places as complex and multi-faceted cultural entities. All too often place marketing and tourism professionals make a reductive and instrumental use of local cultural resources, without entering into a genuine dialogue with the worlds of cultural production, management and policy. This book begins to outline the potential of this dialogue to enrich, refine and make more effective not only place marketing practice, but place development and regeneration strategies more generally. Lastly, I am very pleased that this publication is both the first to be produced by the International Cultural Planning and Policy Unit (previously the Cultural Planning Research Unit, established 1995), and a joint project with Comedia, a constant stimulus for new cultural policy and planning research.

Dr. Franco Bianchini, Director,
International Cultural Planning and Policy Unit

The landscape of place marketing

Mapping the territory

The business of promoting 'places' (towns, cities, regions and countries) is centuries old, from the original Olympic Games to competing Renaissance City states. The last two decades have witnessed a substantial growth in this practice as a response to a more global market place where cities compete not only for tourism, but for the relocation and retention of businesses and to win accolades and competitions like European Capital of Culture, major sports events or global conferences. A new kind of professional marketer has been charged with embodying local identity and promoting it to the rest of the world.

Yet the emerging practice of place marketing shows worrying signs. This new research investigates the content of place marketing messages in promotional literature and reveals disturbing trends. Instead of a dynamic and challenging approach to local character, we are confronted with unrepresentative stereotypes and parodies of the past. Rather than an inclusive methodology that addresses local audiences, it is exclusively outward-looking, thereby ignoring whole sections of the population. Authenticity and reality are substituted for a burlesque caricature of place. The messages follow an insipid formula, which makes it difficult to distinguish one place from another.

Creativity and 'place'

Identity, sense of place and local distinctiveness are key features of the competitive success for places.

This individuality is increasingly associated with cultural vitality. 'Glasgow City of Culture' transformed our perceptions of the city. Rotterdam, once notorious for the roughness of its port area, is now internationally renowned for a visionary approach to architecture and urban development and its hip underground culture. Emscher Park in the Ruhr is a by-word for cultural excellence and experimentation, hosting massively ambitious shows by artists like Christie and Jean Claude (of 'wrapped Reichstag' fame) in previously disused and miserable industrial sites. Huddersfield in West Yorkshire, hit hard by the 1980's textile closures, is regarded as an innovator, leading a vanguard into the territory of new creative industries and innovating in urban development. There is considerable evidence that most place marketing has not kept up with these step-changes, and has chosen an entirely different and disturbing route.

This research project reveals a strong tendency in place marketing literature to focus on a limited view of heritage, with the past mentioned six times as often as the present. Heritage is big business in Britain, but identity is not based on the past alone, it is an evolving process.

An equally worrying trend is to represent 'places' as culturally homogeneous (10.2% of references), and not to acknowledge or recognise diversity (only 3.2%), which can alienate local audiences.

Dead spaces to living places

Making Sense Of Place traces the lineage of place marketing and finds it rooted firmly in product marketing, an essentially reductive process - boiling things down simplistically and seeking common denominators. More used to dealing with inanimate objects, product marketing brings useful experience and analytical tools to the table, but without finding a way of recognising and dealing with the complexity of and variety within places, it remains an inappropriate and limited approach. There is also an important and potentially volatile difference between marketing products and services and marketing something as complex as a 'place'.

Places are made by people, their perceptions and their responses to environmental influences. In a way, a place represents a bundle of ideas that have been put together by different groups, usually over many years even centuries. At times these ideas may appear to be in conflict; places look different depending on how old you are, what your cultural background is, your income level and whether you are disabled. People attach a multi-layered set of identities to places that are significant to them. Where you were born, where you live, where you work, where you felt threatened, where you met a partner. This makes place an extremely complex and multi-faceted concept, not easily reducible, represented or reflected through traditional marketing practice.

The very approach that is making our towns cities and regions successful - the application of creativity, the development of cultural vitality, the celebration of difference - is severely lacking in the practice and literature being used to promote 'places'.

It is as if marketing and promotion are disconnected from the body of activity, development, regeneration and renewal that are energising many localities; the overall 'place-development'.

The research summarised

The research on which this study is based does not pretend to be exhaustive: a sample of 77 tourism and marketing brochures were used. It does not claim to be completely conclusive and clearly some factors merit further study. Yet what the research provides is clear evidence of something wrong, and of some worrying trends and questionable approaches to place marketing practice in the UK.

In summary, it shows a strong and persistent tendency in UK place marketing literature to:

- focus on the past and be generally backward-looking;
- represent places as culturally uniform; and
- not to show diversity, but to promote a similar, bland mix of facilities and attractions for every area.

The kinds of identities being projected are at best partial and at worst completely fictitious. The pages of brochures are crowded with images of the past – 85% of the sample have a heritage theme for the cover, people in historic costume, knights in armour, gentle country peasants and local fisher-folk enjoying a pipe at dusk with their dog on the quayside. This would not be a problem if the images were balanced with others, but generally they are not. The brochures lack a sense of authenticity or reality.

The personality of a place is complex, hard to pin down and, by its very nature constantly shifting and evolving. This does not mean that we can ignore it, or try to create a fictitious one.

Local distinctiveness **- factor X**

Identity is what distinguishes place from place or city from city. It is what provides people with a broader, richly layered sense of that place and what connects them to it, giving them a stake and a sense of ownership. This in turn creates better places. There is evidence (Adams and Ingham 1998) that people are less disaffected and more engaged with the place they live in if this individuality is developed and communicated and if they feel involved.

This can be described as *distinctiveness*, which only occurs when the special features and character of 'place' have been nurtured and used creatively to develop and promote it. It may be a combination of heritage, geography, the economy, a heterogeneous community or a progressive environmental approach.

Whichever, these illusive individual qualities can quite literally transform the economy of an area and the way it is promoted. They can increase employment opportunities by bringing in more businesses and retaining those already present. They can push up property and land values, increasing the return on investment for investors and commercial developers. It can increase tourism and make the place a destination for local people, retaining their spending in the area and increasing inward investment.

Identity, and the way it is handled and promoted, also affords an opportunity for community development initiatives. It can provide a tool for discussing complex local issues and conflict resolution. It can bring in communities from the margins, giving them a stake in the area, giving them a voice. Place marketing can also involve people in participating in projects that not only promote, but actually develop that locality and the network of relationships within it.

So, within place marketing there is the potential for a sophisticated practice that could: give places a competitive edge in the global market place; transform the local economy; increase inward investment and tourism; and develop new and innovative approaches to community development and social inclusion. In short, place marketing could occupy a central position in place development, urban regeneration and renewal. Instead, it is a practice that, with some exceptions, offers up the same mixture of messages for very different places, ignoring creativity and difference, and risking the alienation of local communities often rendering the very places they are promoting unrecognisable to those that live there and to those that visit.

New vistas - shifting the perspective

The vision described for the future of place marketing requires a radically different approach to that usually adopted. It means a complete shift in mind-set, from seeing places as products to be promoted as a series of fictitious features and benefits, towards a practice which views places as living, breathing, cultural entities.

Making sense of place uncovers examples of alternative approaches, both in the UK and continental Europe, pointing to the conclusion that the key to a different kind of place marketing lies in seeing places as living and lived entities, rather than as a set of facilities, landscapes or cityscapes.

Examples include: Barcelona where a complex public art and 'pocket park' scheme has transformed perceptions; Bilbao that, in addition to the Guggenheim, has initiated a long term process of people-focused regeneration; Lille which has changed its potential by re-inventing its city centre; and the Ruhr, transforming an industrial wasteland into a 100 kilometre long cultural trail linked to recreating a modern new technology economy by interestingly re-using old industrial sites.

These examples have been so successful they have catalysed a series of initiatives across Europe, placing the cultural sector at the centre of revitalising and repositioning cities and regions. The research evidence suggests that the UK is slow in grasping these opportunities and, in an increasingly large and crowded market place, UK cities and regions are in danger of under-estimating their potential and so losing their voice.

Place marketing must fundamentally shift its view of place as more than a product or destination. Viewing places as living cultural entities can generate and trigger a more innovative kind of practice.

Planning 'culturally' – an alternative future

Adopting a cultural planning approach to place marketing and promotion will help us innovate, adapt current techniques and develop new ones. This approach can be described as planning culturally, understanding the key features and drivers that shape a place. It is a process that comprehends the symbiotic relationship between people and 'place'; people's cultures shape places, develop industries and transform environments. Conversely, these factors can shape a culture. Taking a cultural approach to marketing also enriches the discipline itself, and the research evidence shows this to be badly needed.

Artists and other 'cultural producers' do not have a monopoly on creativity, but the approach they take to innovation can be adapted and used in a variety of fields, including place marketing. As the artist Paul Klee said "art does not reproduce the visible, it makes visible". Place marketing needs to move from derivative reproduction to revealing the unique, in the same way.

Working across sectoral boundaries, being experimental and original, adopting a more critical, challenging and inquiring approach, putting people at the centre, and developing a deeper understanding of the past, present and future of the place we are promoting, will radically shift current thinking.

Appointing Local Ambassadors

In an age of mass media and complex messages, 'word of mouth' remains an unparalleled form of communication. If we have a bad experience as a customer, we tell up to twenty people; if good, we may tell only five or six. Place marketing needs to turn this basic principle of customer care to its advantage.

We could turn the tables on traditional promotion, making local people into what Charles Landry (1999) has called local Ambassadors for the place instead of just talking about famous people who have lived there. If local residents feel a sense of real pride in the area, they will be the most effective means of communicating a positive image. However, achieving this sense of connectedness and pride is not easy.

It must start by engaging the resident in generating marketing solutions and creating new content for promotional messages. Giving ownership and a sense of control over their own images and representation will result in a commitment to change and the motivation to make it happen. This process enriches the pool of possibilities and ideas for future campaigns.

The beginnings can be seen in the creation of young people's MPs and parliaments across the country. In Birmingham, a committee of young people has been appointed to contribute to discussions about the future planning of the city. Handled imaginatively, this secures commitment and future participation. The Netherfield Marketing Initiative, mentioned in detail later, provided an opportunity for local people to train in marketing skills then offer services within their own estate as part of a regeneration scheme.

Ownership can generate unexpected spin-offs, giving people a stake in their area's future, getting them to help shape it through its own living culture. Local people are permeated by this culture, steeped in the reality of their area.

In moving forward we need a plan to help. Six key actions identified at the end of this book attempt to do this.

Redrawing the map -the six step approach

1. Integration

We need more integrated practice, working with professionals from different disciplines and backgrounds - artists, sociologists, urban geographers, health professionals, the police - and from different sectors. Both the private and public sectors have an equally large stake in the promotional success of a place and they should be working more closely together to achieve this. Integration also means that place marketing cannot be an add-on, it has to be part of the total development process for an area, involved at every stage.

2. Participate to innovate

Opportunities need to be generated for local communities to participate in projects that develop a deeper understanding of the character of their area and help to promote it at the same time. They should be regarded as Ambassadors of their place, and one of its most important promotional assets. This is not just about consultation to achieve a bland consensus. It is about creating a living, breathing promotional campaign which places local people at its heart; so about mobilising local cultural assets and generating 'ideas-banks' for future campaigns.

3. From place marketing to place development

The role and status of place marketing and its professional teams could be greatly expanded to occupy a central point between various agencies, communities and audiences in a place where their function is essentially about communication. Possibilities include bringing in communities from the margins, helping to sift through the issues, finding new ways of enabling people to express their originality, to add to the richness of the 'place' and to promote in different and vibrant ways to entirely new audiences. This shifts the emphasis from place marketing to place development.

4. The right tools for the job: a new place marketer's toolkit

The analytical tools, research and development models needed by this new vanguard of 21st Century marketing professionals will be very different to those provided by the product marketing sector. Some current tools could be adapted, but new approaches to research and evaluation that are more qualitative are required. A radically different approach to the use of imagery and descriptive text is recommended, involving artists, writers and others.

5. Breaking the mould - retraining the professionals

To achieve these new goals, place marketers will need new kinds of training. A marketing background will remain important, but teams could comprise a range of other skills and disciplines. Community development, cultural sector or research-based professions might all feature. A new professional body for place marketers could carry this torch, whilst developing new standards of professional and ethical practice, qualifications and professional development opportunities.

6. Shifting the mind-set: a new definition of place

Finally, we must change, expand and re-conceive our definitions of place. Places are shaped and made by people's actions and by their perceptions. Places are constantly changing and shifting, they are not monolithic and frozen in time. At the core of the identity of 'place' are local people as well as the businesses, facilities and local landscapes. If their knowledge, concerns and imagination are not involved, represented and reflected more fully in place marketing we will be unable to move away from fictitious stereotyping towards a more authentic, diverse and rich set of messages and communications about places.

In conclusion, the book recommends a series of pilot projects that will test and develop some of these ideas, eventually leading to a novel approach to place marketing that will not only make the practice itself more successful but ultimately, make our towns cities and regions better places to visit, work and live.

Exploring the landscape - the research project

Analysis and interpretation

The impetus for the research flowed from a growing realisation of strong examples of rich thinking about place marketing in continental Europe, reflecting a quality of practice rare in the UK.

The research material came from my local Tourist Information Centre. I took a copy of every brochure that they had in stock at the time, 77 in all. The sample therefore only represents one element of available place marketing literature, but nevertheless the most prevalent, most available and most read.

Through content analysis (Krippendorf 1980) this mass of information was scrutinised, to get underneath its skin, beyond the chapter headings and glossy photos to try to establish the real messages.

The analysis was applied in a fairly straightforward way. First, I decided on a number of attributes that I felt would give an indication of what the brochures were telling us about their places. Criticism of place marketing literature is not new, and previous concerns have included: being out of step with local developments; inappropriately representing local people; constantly harking back to the past; and representing places as having only one culture (Erickson and Roberts, 1997). What is new about *Making sense of place* is that it sets out for the first time to provide detailed evidence of what people have been saying for some time.

Past criticisms formed the basis for the research fields (see below) to investigate the attributes and key features of places that were being described in brochures. This included quite simple analyses, such as how many times the past was mentioned compared to the present.

All the brochures were meticulously read through and, using a consistent scoring system, each reference to the chosen attributes marked down.

What I had not expected was that results would so clearly show such a strong bias towards a narrow, historical representation of places.

Keeping score

I set myself a few rules for scoring. If a particular attribute from the list below (e.g. 'the past') was mentioned in the title of a brochure, it scored ten points. If it was mentioned as a chapter heading, it scored five. Any other reference scored one point. Each title, chapter heading and paragraph could only be scored once, unless more than one very distinct reference to a field was made.

Defining the landscape - the research results

Although a follow up study might extend the scope of the results by using additional fields, significant conclusions can be drawn from this research. In addition to the hard statistics and the conclusions, drawn-out into the six-step approach, a number of intriguing and perplexing factors emerged. These could not be recorded in the research fields and are outlined below.

Minority languages

None of the brochures provided information for ethnic minority communities or offered any information in minority languages. This is in stark contrast to information specifically targeted at European visitors and available in French German and Italian. One is left with a sense that it is easier for a French tourist to access information they can understand than it is for, in some cases, large percentages of the local population. Place marketing tends to be externally focused and does not see its own populations as an audience, or as the potential local Ambassadors described earlier. I doubt whether French visitors to Leicester amount to the 30% plus of local Asian communities.

Access and disabilities

Some visitor attractions listed in brochures indicated whether facilities for disabled visitors were available by use of the wheelchair icon. However, beyond this, only one brochure, *Rutland '99*, made a specific reference to local facilities for disabled people. This seems astonishing, not least because a large percentage of older visitors - at whom much of this literature is undoubtedly aimed - will have access and other needs.

The definition of disability used in the brochures is limited to physical access. Estimates for disabled people in the UK put the figures at somewhere between 11-24%, depending on definitions (some people would not regard themselves as disabled and the 'registered' figures do not account for this). Perhaps a quarter of the UK population remain un-catered for in the brochures which is a serious omission.

Film locations

Frequent reference was made to film and TV shot in the area. If the film or programme was well known then the brochure was likely to be built almost entirely around this, in titles like *Herriott Country '99*, or *Shrewsbury - Historic Home of Brother Cadfael*. There is an obvious tourist draw in exploiting this coverage, but it might be regarded as unbalanced and not creating a particularly distinctive sense of locality to totally identify a place with fictional characters.

This persistent trend of relating places to their fictional appearance on the big or little screens, perhaps reflects the way that we, as a society, build, accept and validate identity through the media. The TV or film production is more real to us than the place itself.

The weather

The weather and seasonal change was mentioned a surprising number of times, confirming our British preoccupation. It is perhaps an attempt to reassure foreign tourists that either:

a) the weather is really not that bad; or

b) that the bad weather just adds to the drama and character of the experience (wind-swept moors, etc.).

Religion

Christian religion and traditional moral values were given a high profile, which was unexpected. In contrast, references to minority or alternative religions were scant, though there were some. Christian faith occasionally appeared in the same context as pre-Christian 'Celtic' cultures; the fact that they were non-Christian was not mentioned. This created the same contrast as the lack of reference to minority faiths. The brochures once again miss an opportunity to create depth and richness of message.

Arts and crafts

Mentioned very frequently, but in a slightly banal way (pottery, watercolours, wood turning, textiles) rather than in reference to particular local traditions or skills. The use of arts and crafts in the message content could deliver a sense of local flavour if particular crafts, artists or studios from the area were profiled. The kinds of products displayed were uncontentious, familiar and in no way challenging. A major section of the arts is missing, particularly contemporary arts.

As well as pleasing objects and leisure opportunities, the arts challenge, express and reflect, revealing the otherwise invisible. They are a major economic driver, as the creative industries (turning over £112 billion in the UK per annum) and 'arts quarters' across the UK testify. These were not the arts on display in the brochures.

There is nothing wrong with depicting 'applied' arts and crafts, but there is no counter-balance and no attempt to differentiate area from area. Contemporary arts might be used to develop the 'handwriting' of promotional campaigns.

Lack of change

The past - particularly the medieval period - and a lack of change in the environment is constantly pushed, leaving one feeling that nothing has happened in the last four hundred years. A stable and unchanging Britain floating righteously on a sea of chaos elsewhere is not the Britain I recognise. The vast majority of brochures depict heritage on the front cover, strongly reinforcing the message of the text.

'Memories are made of this'

Storing memories, almost ticking off experiences as if on a list, feature highly. It is as if visiting an area is a kind of investment into a memory bank. There's nothing wrong with that in itself, but it does add to the sense that the present is not part of the picture - we are asked to experience the past in order to create a memory for the future.

Much of the information seems narrowly targeted at the moderately well-off over-50s, playing on the nostalgia for a bygone era, and fomenting sentimental thinking, even perhaps hinting at an intuition of death.

The over fifties are one niche audience, but there are others. While it is difficult to balance one set of communications across different market segments, this approach is too focused. It is easier to achieve this on the web. *Making Sense of Place* is based on print rather than web publications, and further research is needed in the virtual arena. A cursory exploration however reveals the websites of the brochures' producers to be almost entirely the same as the print.

Measuring the contours - the research scores

1. Local Geography/natural environment

Score: 1147 % of total score: 23.7%

2. Local people - friendly

Score: 163 % of total score: 3.4%

3. Local people – other references

Score: 15 % of total score: 0.3%

4. Local culture - diversity

Score: 157 % of total score: 3.2%

5. Local culture - homogeneity

Score: 495 % of total score: 10.2%

6. Local occupations/economy

Score: 179 % of total score: 3.7%

7. The present

Score: 223 % of total score: 4.6%

8. The past/heritage

Score: 1134 % of total score: 23.5%

9. Leisure

Score: 1047 % of total score: 21.6%

10. Uniqueness - non specific

Score: 218 % of total score: 4.5%

11. Uniqueness - specific

Score: 61 % of total score: 0.3%

Framing the view - what do the results mean?

This is not rocket science, yet there is a strong element of objectivity in the scoring method. Indeed the results are quite startling and point to a number of important conclusions. The scores reveal some worrying signals contained within the sample literature demonstrating where the emphasis is being placed in the brochures' messages. Local geography, the past and leisure account for almost 70% of total references, the others almost paling into insignificance by comparison. The message is strong. The priority is a 'natural' environment, which has preserved the past and provides a fixed set of leisure opportunities. The past dominates the present in the text and is even more overbearing in the cover images. Castles, medieval vistas and people in costume are paraded before us in a bizarre pageant. Other issues, people, their changing culture, the emerging economy, even uniqueness are completely secondary.

Local Geography/natural environment

This is the most frequently mentioned field, six times more often than people. It is quite reasonable to assume that visitors will want to experience beautiful scenery, even though the reality may not match the pictures, which often avoid showing the real urban context of the landscape with its ordinary housing, shopping and streetscape. So placing such a strong emphasis on it is 'putting all your eggs in one basket', and casting a shadow over other reasons for visits. Many references to landscape were so general that they quite easily could have been swapped between brochures.

'Spectacular blooms', 'magnificent views', 'beautiful beaches', 'remarkable landscape', 'beautiful surroundings', 'unspoilt landscape', 'natural charm'.

Yet the landscape in Britain is rarely natural, always shaped by people and their activities, and we have an unusual relationship to it. Paradoxically for one of the most urbanised countries in Europe, the British tend to view cities, particularly their centres, as places of dread and the suburbs - where town and countryside meet - are home to the aspirational classes. In many other cities in Europe this situation is reversed and, since medieval times, people have desired to live in the heart of the city, within its walls.

The British view of the countryside swings between an Arcadian idyll where locals are at one with nature, to a suspicion of backwardness, bigotry and animal cruelty.

The landscape is a resource and can be a major attraction, but it does not need to be represented so forcefully, excluding other resources and attractions, and neither does it have to be represented in such a flat and homogeneous way.

The landscape can be interpreted and experienced in unconventional and exciting ways. The Yorkshire

Sculpture Park, at West Bretton near Wakefield, has created a unique relationship between sculpture and the landscape.

Sculpture in the landscape

The Yorkshire Sculpture Park is situated in some of the most spectacular landscape in West Yorkshire. It takes in rugged fields, rolling hills, formal 17th Century gardens and landscaped grounds rumoured to have been designed by Capability Brown.

The landscape is in itself quite breathtaking, although far from natural and shaped by human activity over many centuries. Through the Sculpture Park, a new relationship between people and the landscape has evolved.

The YSP Collections include work from Rodin to Henry Moore to more recent contemporary and conceptual sculptors. Most of this work is sited within the open landscape, at once challenging and changing our perceptions about our environment. The work provides contrasts, stimulation and explanation about the landscape. Henry Moore's work was inspired by this landscape and seeing it in its own habitat enables a new understanding both of the work and of the environment in which it is sited.

This unique approach to revealing the landscape,

digging beneath its surface also makes contemporary sculpture much more accessible. People will encounter it on a walk, a picnic, a day out. It will be a part of their experience, a part of their reason for visiting, unlike a more traditional gallery, and so the sculpture becomes part of their own internal landscape.

It reinforces the lack of insight in these brochures that the Yorkshire Sculpture Park is not given a fuller profile in the accommodation guide for that area.

Local people – friendly; Local people – other references

Local people are referred to in a bland and stereotypical way as 'friendly' - 'the friendly Yorkshireman', 'the cheery Somerset Farmer' - ten times for every one time that there is any reference to any kind of diversity. This is a surprisingly biased and worrying result. It renders places unrecognisable to local people and is extremely partial. It is also not honest. It makes one question whether we believe that visitors only want to be patronised in this way and that, for example, tourists to West Yorkshire are not interested in the large Asian communities or the vibrant festival programmes they inspire like the Bradford Mela.

The Bradford Mela

The Bradford Mela festival is an annual event, which centres around the diverse Asian communities. Growing from a small local authority led spark, it is now a major international tourism attraction for the city.

The Bradford Mela is one of the most popular festivals of its kind in Europe and is responsible for 140,000 visits and very considerable inward investment as a result.

The Mela is mentioned in the brochure that covers Bradford, but only in a cursory way, giving no indication of its local significance or its origins.

Local culture - diversity. Local culture - homogeneity

Three out of every four references to local culture were homogeneous, suggesting that there is only one culture in each place. Some of these references are breathtakingly insipid, particularly when trying to perpetuate the view of an ancient culture.

For example *Sir Gaerfryddin - Camarthenshire 1999* uses 'culture' as a chapter heading, but goes on to explain: "the Welsh culture is inherited from our deep Celtic roots and is evident in our love of music and literature." Rather ironically, the page then goes on to describe the importance of religion in Wales, from a Protestant Christian perspective.

The communities of many Welsh towns and cities - including large ethnic minority communities such as in Cardiff - face real disadvantage and one cannot help but wonder what kind of message this gives to them. It can be of little comfort when struggling financially to know that you are living in the 'Land of Myth and Legend'.

The Celtic tradition is an important feature of Welsh culture, maybe even the central part, but it is condescending at best and exclusive at worst to describe an entire country in this way.

The 'pink pound' - alternative place marketing segmentation

Marketing places as culturally unvaried is not only dishonest, it is also missing a basic marketing opportunity to segment your customers and communicate with them in more personal, richer ways.

London is Britain's most popular tourism destination, not just for those interested in its heritage, but also for those interested in its diverse cultures, for example its clubbing culture and gay community.

Place marketers realised that there was a tourism opportunity here and so have produced specific place marketing communications - print and web based - aimed at gay tourists, aimed at attracting what is referred to as the 'pink pound'.

It requires a different approach to that encountered in the brochures, and appears to have been a success. There are many other distinct communities and groups within any 'place' that can be communicated with, yet our current place marketing approach is, on the whole, unsophisticated and clumsy, and in need of refinement. Instead of depth, colour and texture, our messages are a monotonous semaphore.

Local occupations/economy

There were few references to either of these categories, 3.7% in total, yet where mention was made it did add spice to the brochure and generally referred to a specific local industry or economy, such as fishing in Cornwall and shoe manufacture in Northampton. However the references were scarce and contained little detail.

Interestingly, some brochures for the same area approached their economy in varied ways. Falmouth and South West Cornwall '99 refers to: "archetypal Cornish fishing villages; a cluster of nets, lobster pots and boats."

In contrast, *Inspirational Cornwall '99* has a whole section on contemporary art and the influence of artists like Ben Nicholson, Barbara Hepworth and Bernard Leach have had on the region.

The brochures reviewed for *Making sense of Place* were not inward investment publications. These promote a locality to businesses, rather than potential visitors. They contain information about the local economy, the available workforce and resources, housing and leisure. Elements of this information could be used to expand the unvarying description of 'place' in the brochures.

However, both kinds of brochure promote their message to an external audience; they are outward-facing and have ignored internal, local audiences. The few good examples from the research, (for example 'Bristol Style' in *Bristol City and Countryside,* a youth culture section) spoke simultaneously to both internal and external audiences.

A deeper investigation of the economy and industry of the area in its broadest sense, with related and more creative messages, will greatly enhance the local, personal nature of the literature. Other approaches to using and interpreting local industry have been successful, for example opening disused coal mines as museums and theme parks. Some historic industries are much more troubling and difficult to interpret, but can lead to unique projects.

Challenging the past to change the future

A challenging local industry to explore is Bristol's past role in the slave trade. For many years this went unacknowledged, something too contentious to discuss in the public arena, let alone develop any kind of project around. This has changed with the opening of an exhibition inside Bristol City Museum that describes and interprets this element of the city's past.

The exhibition sits at the heart of an important yet challenging debate about the past that is very much focused on the present. It offers an interactive educational experience for school students, which can facilitate discussion back in the classroom. The centre acknowledges the past and raises important issues about the future. It is a vital part of exploring local culture and yet is also a major tourism attraction, but is not directly referred to in the local brochure.

The present. The past/heritage

For every reference to the present, there are six to the past. Heritage is one of the UK's greatest tourism assets with visits to our 2500 registered museums and other heritage sites totalling more than 100 million annually. Britain's second most popular visitor attraction is the British Museum, with only Blackpool Leisure Beach beating it.

22% of visits to heritage sites in the UK are made by overseas visitors; 59% of all overseas visitors rate museums and heritage as the most important factor in their decision to visit (DCMS 1998). Its therefore not surprising that heritage and the past has a high profile in the literature, however it surely does not need to eclipse the present so comprehensively.

Some brochures take a different approach and stood out from the crowd. *Salisbury and South Wiltshire, The Official Guide*, an area with much to shout about in terms of heritage including Stonehenge, is subtitled *One Foot Firmly in the Present* having realised the limitations of a backward looking approach to local identity. By comparison *Welcome to Wiltshire, the Heart of Wessex* is an archaeological journal, resurrecting the title 'Wessex' after several hundred years, curiously at the same time as the Royal Family following Prince Andrew's and Sophie Rhys-Jones' marriage.

Malverns, Approved Accommodation Guide explained the importance of the past by relating it to the present and then goes on to speak about the future. Culture is invoked as the key to the area's future success. A photograph of ultra modern architecture had the caption "Malvern Theatres - a signpost to the future." Very few brochures took this approach; those that did stood out as more vibrant and interesting, reflecting their mixed localities. There is heritage, but also something going on in the here and now with aspirations for the future.

The focus on the past is a worrying trend that can result in collectively looking back towards some fictitious 'Golden Age' in order to avoid the difficulties and complexities of the present.

Leisure

Leisure had the third highest number of references, 21.6%, next to the past and geography. In one sense this is completely understandable. Visitors will require leisure facilities and this may be a primary motivation for a visit. What these references did not do was create any distinctiveness between the leisure offer of one place and that of another.

Horse riding, cycling, swimming, walking, boating. Everywhere the same. Only rarely were leisure opportunities related to the character of the 'place' its landscape or economy. When this did happen, it set the brochure apart from the crowd. For example, *The North Wales Borderlands* invites us to try tailor-made activity packages connected to the local environment.

Leisure is central to successful place marketing, but so is individuality. Leisure activities can be framed in relation to the locality, its landscape, culture and economy adding to the sense of place. Alternatively, the leisure offer may stand out because it contrasts strongly with its environment in a creative or unusual way.

Escape to *Xscape*

Milton Keynes is renowned for a different and progressive approach to urban development, but even the pioneering founders of the city could not have predicted its latest leisure offer - *Xscape*.

A massive chrome building, nearly two hundred feet high at one end, tapering almost to the ground at the other, it looks like a crashed space ship or something from *Blade Runner*. The building contains an indoor real-snow ski slope.

Built underneath and around this are a multiplex cinema, nightclubs, bars, restaurants, shops, a health club and cafes. It is a complete leisure and retail offer in itself, yet part of a wider picture within the city centre. P. Y. Gerbeau, of Millennium Dome fame, has recently been appointed as the Managing Director. Xscape has been extremely popular, particularly with young people, and has contributed something new to the uniqueness and distinctiveness of Milton Keynes, whose destination the offer has gone completely beyond natural and geographical limitations to include kind of skiing and snowboarding you really have to wrap up for. This provides another interesting dimension for local brochures to explore.

Uniqueness - non specific. Uniqueness – specific

Only one in every five references to uniqueness were qualified in any way. It seems that places are just 'unique' which we should accept unquestioningly. I cannot see a reason for not qualifying these claims if it were possible. Where uniqueness was specific, it tended to be about the landscape or the past; 'the unique panorama', 'our unique heritage'. In a sense, this is all true. Everywhere is unique, but you would not think so from reading these brochures.

The brochures have missed the point. What is important is generating a sense of difference for the reader, not just claiming to be unique and hoping it will be believed. The brochures confuse distinctiveness and uniqueness. Everywhere is unique in some form, but it is the substance of that uniqueness, the way it is explored, enhanced, developed and interpreted that makes a place 'distinctive'.

Halifax and Batley in West Yorkshire are both unique, like every other small town in the area. Batley is distinctive for a number of reasons, partly because of its regeneration of local mills like *Skopos* that has been successful enough to attract specialist outlets such as Europe's largest Japanese antique dealer, also because of the innovative approach taken to local renewal and reduction of crime and fear of crime by incorporating public art into these schemes.

Halifax also has many outstanding features, including Dean Clough, a regenerated industrial warehouse complex from the last century that is now a thriving cultural hub, home to galleries, arts facilities and creative industries. These kind of features add greatly to the sense of texture and richness of the locality. They need revealing within promotional messages, adding depth and reality.

Glasgow - unique and distinctive

When Glasgow became European City of Culture in 1990, there were those who could not quite believe it. Glasgow had a reputation for high unemployment, crime, heavy drinking and gang fighting. Glasgow also had, however, a fantastic cultural wealth and distinguished heritage that was simply not known very well outside the area.

The City of Culture programme allowed Glasgow the opportunity to package its cultural resources in an innovative way, giving the city a distinctive and completely new profile. Although the programme has been criticised, particularly in relation to its community development outcomes, it transformed perceptions of the city perhaps more than any other European City of Culture has so far done. The city moved from a position of being *unique*, in some good and not so good ways, to being *distinctive* and being repositioned in people's mindsets, reinforced through tourism literature, as a centre for cultural excellence and a city worthy of exploration.

From images to icons

Taking in the view

Most brochure images were photographic, with some drawings and watercolours. The imagery is as troubling as the text. Many are obviously, stiffly posed, drenched in the past and focused on the landscape. The cover pages particularly reinforce the heritage message of the brochure's interiors.

We had hoped to print a number of images here, but several of the brochures' authors (usually an agency or local authority) were reluctant to allow this and so we abandoned the idea. They were worried that they would be placed in a critical context, but such a defensive stance does not suggest conviction or pride.

Instead, we have put together a brief imagery survey of four brochures, selected randomly from the sample. In addition, the occurrence of heritage imagery on the cover page of all brochures has been surveyed.

Imagery survey results

Sixty six out of seventy seven– a staggering 85.7% - of all the sample brochures carried predominantly heritage based imagery on the cover. This completely overshadows any other references and reinforces the nostalgic, hackneyed and fictitious way in which places are represented as heritage theme parks.

The original research fields were designed in relation to text, rather than images, and so some fields remain empty, like uniqueness, which cannot really be judged from an image.

1. Local Geography/natural environment
Score: 199 % of total score: 42%

3. Local people - friendly
Score: 31 % of total score: 6.6%

2. Local people – other references
Score: 10 % of total score: 2.1%

4. Local culture - diversity
Score: 4 % of total score: 0.8%

5. Local culture - homogeneity
Score: 10 % of total score: 2.1%

6. Local occupations/economy
Score: 12 % of total score: 2.5%

7. The present
Score: 22 % of total score: 4.7%

8. The past/heritage
Score: 103 % of total score: 21.8%

9. Leisure
Score: 82 % of total score: 17.4%

10. Uniqueness - non specific No score
11. Uniqueness – specific No score

This reinforces the findings of the content analysis survey. There is an obsession with the past, regimented leisure opportunities and rural landscape. Other references are overcast by the shade of these giant preoccupations.

Imagery has not been explored in a challenging or enquiring way. It is mainly rustic and steeped in the past, emphasising the lack of sincerity and authenticity. They images are institutional and monosyllabic. It is not easy to communicate the complex nature of any place simply, but this does not mean it is impossible or worth the reward.

Symbols and signs

We are adept at grasping complex ideas from simple communications. Certain symbols – flags, religious imagery, mythical images, company logos – all carry weighty concepts within them, yet are easily recognisable.

This is what Landry (2001) has called the *iconic trigger*, a simple message that conveys complexity in one image, or just a few words.

The 'Forces of Light'
In Helsinki, Charles Landry worked to identify how the city's cultural resources and traditions could be mobilised. Visiting during the harsh Finnish Winter, he observed how traditions shifted with the seasons.

Seasonal Affective Disorder – a depressed condition believed due to prolonged periods of darkness – was referred to constantly. This seemed counterbalanced by traditions involving light: candlelight, fire and the city's growing niche economy around lighting design and manufacture.

Valon Voimat – The Forces of Light – started in 1994, began originally as a two week festival and is now a powerful local agent for tourism, economic development and social cohesion. Building on the bleak winter, the programme utilises a cultural planning approach to turn the darkness into a strength. The idea is simple, but powerfully iconic; in three or four words it speaks volumes, it is an *iconic trigger*, not just for the Finns, but for everyone.

In Helsinki the iconic trigger was not just an image, it involved a subtle shift in perception. The approach built on local traditions and cultural resources, it was feature of the city's personality, rooted in its unconscious.

Beacon-concepts

The product marketing approach to communication evidenced by these brochures is not working. Instead of attempting 'iconic communication' and dealing with the complex in creative ways, it is simply ignored. We are asked instead to accept a counterfeit pastiche of heritage and landscape like a droning monologue from one brochure to the next. Working with artists, writers and other 'cultural interpreters', we should seek out these iconic triggers in our localities, understand and build on them to generate a vibrant chorus instead.

The Helsinki 'Forces of Light' festival is a beacon-concept, illuminating a new path to discovering and interpreting identity. Rather than taking a birds-eye view of a locality, a city or a region, identity is far more likely to be gleaned from close contact on the ground. The collectors and interpreters of identity – marketing agencies, cultural institutions, artists, academics – need to burrow into the local soil, uprooting and unearthing features and traditions, new or old. Identity cannot be designed, but it can be exposed, explored and expressed.

We badly need a new depth of message, icons imbued with personality, reflecting the psyche of an area, communicating simply. To have meaning and bring them closer to reality, these messages must resonate with the fundamental, common experiences of local people.

Scoping the problem

From brochures to visits

Reading the brochures I began to experience a blurring sensation. With few exceptions, they all began to sound the same. Everywhere: is unique but we don't know why; preserves the past and has had little development since the 16th Century; has the same beautiful landscape; and offers the same range of leisure facilities. It is as if someone has decided that this is all people are interested in and so has used all these aspects in all the publicity.

Together, local geography/natural environment; the past/heritage; and leisure accounted for 70% of the total references scored. A 'natural' environment that has preserved the past and provides endless leisure opportunities is the priority. Other features - people, culture, the economy, even uniqueness - are a remote second.

Rather than creating a range of consumer choices, this approach leaves little to choose between places. Describing holidays in this way is not new. It is what Center-Parcs and Butlins have attempted trying to achieve a reliable standard of experience at every venue in the same way as MacDonalds does in its fast food outlets. There's nothing wrong with this: both these companies have allowed people to access experiences they could never have afforded otherwise. Yet places, localities, cities and regions are different to this.

Places are homes, economies and, importantly, the centre or locus of identity and perhaps pride. They cannot be controlled like a leisure park, they have a life and character of their own and do not merely exist to serve the holiday and leisure needs of outsiders.

What makes a place truly interesting and worthy of a visit is its individuality and cultural richness, the things that make it a complete contrast to anywhere else. Representing places as lacking diversity not only makes them less interesting, but is misleading, perhaps damaging and even counter productive, if the aim is to attract new audiences.

Direct place marketing?

What matters most in marketing terms is whether this approach works, and I have found scant evidence. One study, *Beautiful South Lead Generation Campaign* (Southern Tourist Board 1998), is quite detailed.

Promotional brochures advertising accommodation in Buckinghamshire were mailed to 735,000 people. Of these 694 were interviewed over the phone - a substantial enough sample. 14% of respondents had travelled to Buckinghamshire and 3% had stayed overnight, however, only 1% had used the brochure to book accommodation. This is close to an acceptable conversion rate for what is essentially a direct marketing exercise. However, these brochures are expensive and often subsidised by the public purse. The low conversion to sales plus the unrepresentative nature of the brochures compounds their inability to speak simultaneously to internal and external audiences.

The primary objective of the brochures analysed was to generate visits, in some cases to create hotel bookings. The above research suggests they are not particularly successful at achieving this. When it is so difficult to distinguish between 'places' in the literature, people have to base their decisions about where to go on something. Most likely it will be because they have visited before or have heard good 'word of mouth'. This makes the brochures at best a guide for people who are already half way down the ladder of decision making and it is questionable to spend so much on publications that may, in reality, not have much influence on decisions to visit. The expenditure could be justified if the brochures took a more inventive approach, influencing decisions, speaking to wider audiences.

As Forrester notes, in marketing in general and, it seems, place marketing in particular, there is a reluctance to spend money on rigorously examining the effectiveness of promotion.

"The advertising industry spends two or three percent of its gross dollar volume on what it calls 'research' and even if this were really true research, the small amount would be surprising. However, probably no more than one fifth of one percent of total advertising expenditure is used to achieve an enduring understanding of how to spend the other 99.8 percent."

(Forrester, 1991; p613)

So, we do not really know if this approach works, and there is some evidence that it does not and insufficient research to establish whether it does.

From products to places

At this point in the research, I faced a fundamental question: why place marketing literature is so keen to represent places in this bland and unchallenging way.

The answer lies in the origins and evolution of place marketing practice, which are firmly rooted in the traditions and value systems of product marketing. Marketing has been with us for centuries. It perhaps only became a distinct professional practice with a set of theories and analytical tools in the 1950's with the post-war consumer goods boom, in attempts to differentiate products and provide a competitive edge. Product marketing has developed a great deal since then, formalising and standardising techniques and approaches through training, membership bodies and qualifications. However, in one essential respect, marketing remains the same; it is focused mainly around manufactured goods and services - 'products'.

It is undoubtedly useful to think about marketing tools like 'product life-cycles', 'buyer-behaviour', 'features and benefits', and 'mind-sets', no matter what you are trying to market, but it is probably not possible to import these wholesale from product marketing to place marketing practice, when places are so multi-faceted.

The threat these techniques pose to place marketing far outweighs the help they potentially offer. This is because product marketing is a reductionist practice that constantly boils everything down, simplifies and reduces. This is not an appropriate way to deal with the vast experiential range the deep identity of a place represents. Crucially product marketing deals with inanimate objects, as opposed to dynamic, evolving and difficult ideas. This accounts for the unexciting sameness in the literature, presuming a target audience of mainly fifty plus, with disposable income and presenting them with a monotonous treadmill of nostalgia, leisure and recreation. Conversely, the target segment might be described as disinterested in authenticity, the real character and gritty history of the area, which reveals just how patronising these messages can seem.

I found little evidence of research to back these assumptions. An enquiry to the British Tourist Authority turned up a handful of projects, including the above. Whether research or assumption based, this narrow audience focus needs challenging.

Instead of offering visitors a menu of choice rooted in reality, this product led approach based on assumptions results in a burlesque parody of the area's history and resources.

The central dilemma is that places are multiform, cultural entities and the limited product based mindset to marketing them can not be successfully sustained over time. The communicators seem unable to grasp and convey complexity in the iconic sense.

I don't recognise my city!

A product marketing approach to places can be divisive, excluding whole sections of the community paradoxically rendering places unrecognisable to local people, creating a source of disaffection and alienation. It appears at times as if it reflects an excluding and controlling voice of authority that ignores the present and harks back to a fictitious past when everyone knew their place.

How many of us would actually recognise the places we live in from these brochures if the place names were removed. The example of *Leicestershire 1999 - The Real Surprise* shows how entire sections of the population might fail to recognise the place they live in.

Leicestershire 1999, the real surprise!
This brochure is not exclusively about the city of Leicester, but focuses on it in the literature and photographic images.

The brochure contains a surprise, and this is the apparently invisible one-third of the population who are from Asian communities. Two indirect mentions are made: one to a Saree shop, which was pictured; and one to the Divali festival, with a civic building draped in lights. There is also a photograph of an African Caribbean carnival. No specific references to the Asian community are made and there are no images of Asian people.

There may be reasons that led to these choices in the brochure's production, yet the message of the finished article is potentially very difficult. Other brochures carry the same message and can been seen as: non-representative; excluding; patronising; or even inflammatory.

In pure marketing terms, it ignores the tourism potential delivered by the local Asian population. For example, Bradford's annual Asian 'Mela' festival is one of the most popular events of its kind in Europe, attracting a significant portion of its 140,000 visitors from the Asian sub-continent, providing much needed inward investment.

Part of the issue is the way in which the 'marketing' process defines its customers. One can only deduce that the customer focus is on people over 50 with disposable income from outside the area and with a fixed and limited view of culture, leisure and entertainment. And one questions whether these people really exist. There are many other customers such as the overlapping communities of interest that share the space being marketed. These communities also have a stake in the success of a place marketing campaign and can make or break it in-spite of the marketer's best efforts. Place marketing that generates a sense of local pride is far more effective because it mobilises local residents as advocates, what Charles Landry has called "the ambassadorial role of the resident....the best marketing device a city can have." (1999, p3).

Communicating with these varied audiences must be more than simply informing them that a promotional campaign is taking place. A two way process is essential, not necessarily to build a consensus - a common misunderstanding in consultation - but to generate engagement and to create an ideas bank that can be used to enrich the campaign. Marketing professionals may have technical skills, but they do not have a monopoly on good ideas.

The research revealed the literature to be largely out of step with the present focus of life and vitality of a given area. Not only does this lead to the literature being grey, it misses a real trick. It does not mobilise the cultural assets and resources of an area - beyond facilities or events, including its creativity, energy, ingenuity and distinctiveness - and use these as a promotional tool. To do this effectively, place marketing and promotion must be directly connected to the development of that place, whether to regeneration and renewal schemes, or simply to shared aspirations. Campaigns which miss this have a hollow ring and fool few, least of all local residents, as Glasgow discovered in its infamous *Glasgow' Smiles Better* Campaign, that was successful in some respects, yet alienated many locals. Place marketing connects to place development.

A second and more fundamental issue is what perception of a city is being generated. There is a growing tendency to view cities as organic, cultural entities in the West, as opposed to an industrial view of cities as machines.

Depending on which view is taken different sets of conclusions about urban problems or potential are reached. If the machine view is prevalent when something is not working, we might assume a part is broken and needs replacing, or that there is a mechanical error and that with the right housing, a new bypass or pedestrianisation the problem will pass. Yet this is by no means the full picture.

Considering a city as an organic cultural entity helps us to think about it in more comprehensive terms: Its health; learning needs; growth patterns; atmosphere; identity; quality of life; and what will make it thrive. Whilst a more complex model and more difficult to apply than its production oriented predecessor the results speak for themselves. The use of cultural activity as: a tool for urban development; regeneration; economic renewal; and therefore as a Unique Selling Point for place marketing campaigns has had resounding success.

Huddersfield - mining a seam of creativity

The Huddersfield Creative Town Initiative is one of a handful of projects that has earnestly put into practice the cultural planning approach to urban development. Funded by the European Commission as one of a series of Urban Pilot Projects, the Creative Town Initiative as an attempt to revitalise the area by tapping into its creativity.

Through developing training programmes, incubator units and a series of new networks for development and distribution, the project created a strong local creative industries cluster with the aim to develop and retain local talent, creativity and innovation.

Phil Wood, the project Director, saw this as an extension of Huddersfield's past, building on the ingenuity of residents. "Now that the coal's gone from Huddersfield, this is the seam that we have to mine." (1999, p2). The town's slogan *Strong heart, creative mind* reflects the approach.

Project evaluation shows the scheme has been successful locally, but its influence has not ended there. It has inspired administrations and individuals to think differently all over Europe, to expand their thinking and to take a more culturally focused approach to urban renewal.

The Huddersfield Example is remarkable for the way it built on local identity. Instead of an imitative idea, it sought to identify local assets and build on local strengths that people in Huddersfield could recognise, inspiring and raising their aspirations. It assessed, in short, the cultural factors that shape what Huddersfield really is and used that knowledge to motivate local people to become involved.

Success stories like this have begun to reposition the cultural sector to a central position where urban issues become cultural issues; and where 'planning' becomes 'cultural planning'.

" Any form of urban planning is today, by definition, a form of cultural planning in its broadest sense, as it cannot but take into account people's religious and linguistic identities, their cultural institutions and lifestyles, their modes of behaviour and aspirations, and the contribution they make towards the urban tapestry -"

(Worpole, K. & Greenhalgh, L. , 1999, p 4)

They then set out the ingredients for a rich urban tapestry. By sharp contrast, the research literature feels more like a mass produced nylon bedspread. This emphasises the inappropriateness of taking a limited product marketing approach to place marketing which may be fine for products, even complex ones, but cannot be transferred wholesale to the promotion of the complexities of 'place'.

The right tools for the job?

There are several standard tools of marketing analysis that are commonly adapted to serve the needs of different marketing sectors (e.g. service marketing), although they originate with product marketing. These tools are even adapted to disciplines such as fundraising. They include: the product life-cycle (different strategies for new, mature or declining products); the General Electric Portfolio Matrix (discussed later); diffusion and innovation models (new products appealing to different audiences than tried and tested ones); and models of buyer behaviour (how people buy and what affects their decisions). These tools form the bedrock of product marketing and they are all useful and have revolutionised the approach of many businesses.

Some models have been adapted for place marketing and promotion, but they seem, with notable exceptions, quite inappropriate for dealing with the complexities of place, human personality and human behaviour. The exceptions include the various models of buyer behaviour and lifestyle analysis (examining clues in people's lifestyle about what will make particular products appealing), perhaps the only real attempt by the wider marketing community to get to grips with the subtleties of human behaviour.

These models have generated techniques such as psychographic segmentation (close to a psychological profile of different customer groups), attempting to refine the targets (or segments) for marketing communications. The Tesco loyalty card is a remarkable example of how well this process can be managed in relation to products.

The Tesco loyalty card

Tesco was one of the first major companies to take loyalty cards and reward schemes with the seriousness they deserve and it has given them a retail market lead. The Tesco loyalty scheme is complex and represents a pinnacle of direct marketing in the product field in the UK at the time of writing. Using the card saves money and results in rewards. It tracks every item purchased and, together with postcode information, allows Tesco to build up a comprehensive profile of you as a shopper, giving clues about your lifestyle, and perhaps elements of your personality. Using this information, Tesco mail a loyalty magazine to its card-carrying customers. However, they do not all receive the same magazine. Tesco actively manages around 200 separate market segments, producing more than 200 different versions of the magazine tailored to meet the profiles of their customers. In direct marketing terms, this is a phenomenal feat. It is still a far cry from communicating with people as individuals, but ahead of anything the public sector currently has to offer.

Local authorities, regeneration agencies and others continuously communicate with residents about the future of their towns and cities. There are moves to make consultation more interactive, more participatory and more inclusive. It is interesting to think what a public-private sector interface might achieve in terms of communication if it could apply the expertise and the technology of the Tesco example.

Although the Tesco example remains a reductionist approach reflecting a need to pigeonhole, it represents progress. It is helpful to think about different messages for different audiences, but there is an important distinction between product and place.

Place, identity and self

Identity as a commodity

Our clothes, house, car and other goods have important roles in confirming our identity, expressing our differences and similarities. They represent what Pierre Bourdieu calls our cultural capital. But the place in which we are born or live, or the community to which we choose to belong (country, region, ethnic community) will always be more important in defining our self than any product. This is why place marketing has to take a far more sophisticated approach and remains currently an under-developed discipline. It must consider issues about identity in a way that is different and even at odds with other marketing practices.

Crucially product marketing deconstructs identity, whereas in place marketing, the identity *is* the product, which cannot be broken down easily into simplistic elements

Philip Kotler, marketing guru from a product marketing background, has been very influential in place marketing and has written widely. His work takes a product oriented approach to places.

"places are, indeed, products, whose identities and values must be designed and marketed."

(Kotler. 1993, p11)

Whilst there are merits in thinking about places in this way, particularly in relation to promotional campaigns, the imposition of values and identities can be problematic.

Building on Kotler's approach and seeking out the richness of character that exists in any town or city increases the depth and texture of promotional messages and runs less risk of alienating local people. Harnessing and tapping into identity as seen in Lille, the Ruhr, Huddersfield and elsewhere can be the beginning of: social; cultural; and economic transformation. Even in new towns, traditionally and somewhat sadly regarded with suspicion in the UK, identity can be drawn out.

Milton Keynes - Cultural Planning at the heart of the city

Milton Keynes is an unusual city. Misunderstood by the ignorant and those who have never visited, it was in its day a leading-edge and successful experiment in connecting new kinds of urban design with social and cultural development; a kind of urban laboratory.

Benefiting from a strong local loyalties, a can-do attitude and a pioneering spirit, Milton Keynes is set to once again take centre stage in new kinds of urban development. Urban consultants EDAW were appointed by English Partnerships and Milton Keynes Council to review the masterplan for the large city centre. Built from scratch, the centre is incomplete and faces issues around transport and access, public space and inclusion. Built from scratch, the centre is incomplete and faces issues around transport and access, public space and inclusion. Much of the current centre is indoor shopping pace, privately owned.

EDAW's plans will revolutionise the centre. Creating a series of new quarters, civic spaces, a knowledge and enterprise area, business hub and mixed-use residential area, they have taken a bold approach. This is something that could probably only happen in a new town, where - quite literally - green fields are still waiting for development.

However, the real difference between this and other similar projects is that Cultural Planning was included in the project brief for EDAW, who brought in Charles Landry and artist Thomas Heatherwick to work with the team. This meant that culture, in its broadest sense, was at the heart of the new proposals. An enquiring and innovative approach was adopted by the project team, who sought ideas from the community during extensive consultation.

The result is a visionary 25 - 30 year development framework which, once again, positions Milton Keynes as the kind of urban laboratory that makes new discoveries about how we live and how cities can work better.

New tools are needed to enable the place marketer to achieve the aspirations for towns and cities.

Place marketing is hamstrung from contributing more effectively to economic, social and cultural development because of the limited and inappropriate range of its tools, like trying to make a Chippendale chair with an axe or carve marble with a sledgehammer. The tools are not sensitive to the needs of the job. New tools for an imaginative kind of urban development have been considered (Landry 2000). This thinking represents a considerable step forward from the current position, yet is very simple.

Shifting perspective is a key concept. Trying literally to view the city through someone else's eyes; a child, a woman, a tourist, a refugee. For example, I was speaking recently to a local Councillor about an accident blackspot on a housing estate. She told me that no-one could understand why accidents kept happening involving children. There were no bushes and the view seemed clear. Suddenly, someone realised. They were all asked to crouch down and try to cross the road, literally at the height of a young child. There was an unusual camber to the road which obscured the view. Without trying to see the problem literally from a child's perspective, it would have remained a puzzle.

Ways of seeing - present reflected in the past

New Zealand is an increasingly successful tourist destination. It has re-conceived its offer to include its rich heritage, fantastic scenery, arts and film production and a world-class reputation for extreme sports. This is clearly represented visually, both in the arts and the literature, and although this highlights conflict it has contributed to the popularity of New Zealand.

The film, *Once Were Warriors (Lee Tamahon, 1995)*, is at once a grim and yet somehow optimistic exploration of modern-day Maori culture. It begins with a pretty gritty and stark look at one families attempt to cope, but ends by trying to connect the present with the past, by young Maoris integrating their cultural heritage and roots with their present.

The New Zealand author was also the producer of a ground breaking book called *Cook's Sites: revisiting history* (Thomas, N. & Adams, M. 1999). This book explored the connection between the perceptions of the first Europeans arriving in New Zealand and how its present communities see their land. The first Europeans brought artists with them, to record the landscape and its people. In an interesting and innovative move, the book's authors returned to the sites of these original sketches and recorded them again, as photographs. These images, placed next to the original sketches, are striking. Where lively Maori communities once existed, picnic and barbecue sites now surround monuments, not to those communities, but to the European settlers.

Although the book is challenging and critical, it opens up a new kind of debate about places, perceptions and tourism. It somehow increases one's engagement with the landscape and its inhabitants. In a sense, this is what art history or film criticism does. Far from wrecking an experience or overtaxing us, this kind of background knowledge only ever serves to increase understanding, enjoyment and appreciation. This book does exactly that, in a direct way through the use of these images. It is interesting to imagine how this principle might be applied to place marketing literature in the UK.

Renaming issues, concepts, services or challenges can also shift perspective. Shifting the emphasis from 'housing' to 'habitat' is one of the examples Landry, quoting Greenhalgh (Worpole and Greenhalgh 1999) uses. This allows thinking to expand to include the whole area; shops, amenities, parks, local networks and relationships. By taking a broader view, it places the issue in another context so opening up possibilities and solutions that simply were not present before.

Place marketing should adopt this type of thinking in order to develop tools that will be fit for purpose and measure up to the varied and shifting demands of dealing with the complex and multi-layered identities of place.

Digging at the roots – identity uncovered

Identity is central to psychoanalysis and sociology and greater use of this knowledge should be made by place marketers. In psychoanalysis, it is primarily the individual's relationship to other individuals and to themselves and their own past that is examined, whereas sociology primarily deals with individuals in their wider group or social-relationship context.

Psychoanalysis gives us two important ideas that relate to identity: the *unconscious* - that there is an unseen world within us that moves and motivates us; and *therapy* - that a particular kind of relationship and process can reflect that unconscious back to us, enabling a fuller personal understanding. Similarly inhabitants of an area hold tacit and implicit knowledge about their place which needs unlocking.

In considering how these are ideas relevant to place marketing, it is interesting to speculate what the *unconscious* of a place might be, and how that relates to its character. This will reveal the difference between official and unofficial versions of how a place is represented. The official version is the bland, backwards looking model encountered in the research. The unofficial may be a set of more chaotic but energetic views, positive and negative, held by individuals and communities.

The official view tends to censor the unofficial, even rendering it meaningless. Not listening to and acknowledging other views can lead to tension and conflict. The example of Bradford raises an interesting and important point.

Bradford, re-branded as Leeds?

Bradford in West Yorkshire, like many other UK cities, has experienced a declining local economy and a degree of unrest between local communities; as the large local Asian population has felt excluded and unrepresented. Ironically, at the end of a hugely successful festival focusing on ethnic diversity and inter-cultural communication, a wave of violence erupted in part of the city. Blown out of proportion by the media, the incident attracted a provocative response by Central Government.

The response, with some local backing, was to suggest that Bradford merges with Leeds, currently experiencing a real economic boom. A bizarre example of a product led approach to place. The suggestion seems to have been made from 'branding' perspective; "lets re-brand Bradford as Leeds and things will improve, more businesses will buy in and more people will visit". However, such a move could also be read as a kind of draconian punishment; "you've failed at being Bradford, so we're going to turn you into Leeds!"

Whatever is happening in Bradford, and whatever the actual causes, it is a real place with a rich and mixed cultural history and identity, from the Bronte sisters to the Asian Mela festival; from the National Museum of Film and Photography to the Hockney Gallery. Another reading of the current situation might be that people are desperate to be properly recognised as part of the overall identity of the area. If so, losing that identity altogether could be disastrous representing the opposite of what is needed: projects and opportunities to participate that reflect, explore and celebrate the diverse, multi-layered senses of identity and culture in the area, building a 'sense of place'.

Place marketing could evolve a kind of practice that was inclusive of other views; that, like the therapist, helps release hidden energies in a positive and constructive way.

The implication is that any promotional message about a 'place', whether inclusive or not, powerfully reflects the social structures that created it, and this is revealed by analysing the message's content. Therefore, the relationship between the promoting agency and the 'place' being promoted is essential; in the end 'the truth will out'.

The conventional and unvarying nature of the research literature seems to reflect a desire for a simple set of local relationships and a common cultural identity, harking back to an imagined period when everyone new their place. The large number of references to the past compared to the present suggests this. Such claims are fictitious as the UK has a rich and differentiated cultural past with moments of conflict and cohesion in interplay.

A new approach to place marketing means changing the relationships with and between communities in that place. If this happened place marketing literature could carry new and powerful messages about the relationships. It could draw on these local cultural resources to create a sense of distinctiveness in its messages, a real unique selling point, allowing it to stand out from the crowd.

This 'sense of place' can help people to feel more included, more rooted.

"The fostering of a sense of place will work against feelings of dispossession and alienation"

(Adams and Ingham, 1998, p5)

As a consequence the product-oriented approach and Kotler's ideas in particular must be regarded as suspect. The notion of designing identities for places should be rejected as in the end it leads to disaffection; produces untruthful literature that is even offensive to some; and there is insufficient evidence that it works. This is a key issue in the current English regional debate.

Identity in the regions

Since beginning this research work, the Regional Development Agencies (RDA) in England have come into full effect, along with their cultural counterparts, the Regional Cultural Consortiums. This has raised important and difficult issues about regional identity in England, and whether it exists.

England has strong regional areas - Yorkshire is an example - but these exist within a well defined national framework. Elsewhere in Europe, like Italy, regions are stronger and more identified with than nation. Projects with the title national are unlikely to succeed in Italy, so closely are people allied to their region.

The regional layer of government in England is recent and imposed, following administrative boundaries rather than areas with coherent regional character. Far from identifying with these, many local residents are unaware of them.

The regions are not culturally distinctive. Of course there are distinct cultures within them, but these do not relate to the imposed boundaries. Perhaps regional identity cannot be wholly shared, but must remain fragmented and eclectic. However, the RDAs have realised that identity is a key success factor for them. Economically driven, they still understand that identity and distinctiveness, linked to local culture, is essential if they are to be competitive. Shared environments, histories and futures may be sources of regional identity. Paradoxically this investigation may reveal coherent regions whose boundaries are different to those prescribed by government.

The new regions face a huge challenge in developing and promoting their individuality. To risk a pretence of identity would be disastrous and transparently fake, probably alienating everyone. However, this is also a huge opportunity. Taking the approach outlined in *Making Sense of Place*, regional bodies could be the catalyst for a new kind of place marketing, closely linked to place development and regeneration.

The value of identity

An important issue that connects local identity to renewal is its relationship to land and property values. The private sector is deeply involved in urban renewal and regeneration, especially in terms of the built environment. Companies responsible to their shareholders must achieve a financial return on their investment to justify this involvement, yet the private sector is increasingly concerned with issues about local identity. There is a significant relationship between identity, sense of place and the distinctiveness it brings, and property and land values.

Identity and distinctiveness is best drawn out, built upon and promoted in an inclusive way, requiring community participation. This can protract the development process, affecting financial returns, so we should ask why would investors be interested.

The four main factors that affect the capital value of a property development are: 1. Annual revenue (rent), 2. Cost of development (build costs), 3. Investment yield, 4. Timing (letting void).

Rental levels are linked to competition in the market place, location, the building specification, design quality and a building's distinctive, special features. The moment when income is received on completion of the project is crucial; any delay will lead to an 'income void'. The build-cost is a major factor, but does not necessarily vary with location. Short-term thinking, cutting corners and reducing design quality can all ultimately lead to a lower return on investment. The investment yield - the rate of return on the investment through lettings - is based on professional assessments regarding the type of property (office/retail), 'marketability' of the building (location, design quality and specification), and the likelihood of securing a quality tenant. Getting this mix wrong can be disastrous for investors.

"These factors are linked to 'marketability'. If the scheme is not addressing the needs of the market, say it is in a location unpopular for office occupiers, the likelihood of achieving a secure level of income is weakened together with the income void period increasing. This will negatively impact on the investment yield which in turn will reduce the capital value of the scheme. This can also impact on the residual land value."

"Location, location, location" is the clarion call of the property industry. But of course more than one location may be able to offer these incentives.

"The primary factors for selecting a new business location include the availability of a qualified or trainable workforce, access to transportation corridors, proximity to customers and affordability. Whilst issues relating to quality of life don't always appear in the upper rankings at the outset, once a shortlist of locations has been identified, quality of life factors and the distinctiveness of building takes on a much greater significance."
(Interview with John Lewis, Project Director, English Partnerships)

Identity and individuality are strong factors in the decision making process for business locations. They are therefore linked to the developers ability to lease or sell property quickly, maximising income and reducing any letting void.

Bluewater, shopping as a cultural experience?
Bluewater is an acclaimed landmark and hugely successful Shopping Centre in Dartford developed by the Australian company Lend Lease one of the world's largest developers. Here stone and metal carved historic themes are infused throughout the centre on balustrades, friezes, plinths or as part of facias or fountains seeking to add depth and a

thematic drive to the shopping experience. The images show a baker, a welder, hatmakers, coopers and all kinds of making activities that no longer exist in a retail environment as well as uplifting poems so projecting an image of nostalgia for a world long gone. Incorporated too is a branch of the Natural History Museum providing a dinosaur experience as well as a learning centre and even their Costa Coffee shop intersperses its muzac with rapid bursts of Italian language lessons. The intention of Lend Lease is to lift aspiration yet the overall atmosphere remains one of selling.

Created in a redundant chalk-pit, it includes more than 300 units within a unique and highly stylised retail destination, attracting in excess of 1.7 million shopping trips per month. The concept designer, Eric Kuhne, conceived Bluewater as a destination that reflects the areas heritage, promotes identity, pride and a sense of community ownership. Artists have worked alongside developers to integrate both the fabric of the building and the experience of being in it with the local environment. This generates a sense of reality and local roots that many shopping centres lack. A creative and insightful view on how to maximise the return on investment has been taken. Many of the features aim to increase the customers dwell-time, for example shadow free lighting in car parks, as research identified women curtailing shopping trips to avoid returning to cars in the dark.

The ability to attract and retain key staff members is a critical issue for businesses in choosing a location. Quality of life includes: availability and affordability of housing; retail variety; cultural facilities; school quality; recreation and leisure facilities; and low crime rates. These all add to the individual character of an area and it is clear that local identity impacts directly on two key economic issues: property values; and business relocation and retention.

Defining the solution

Globally competitive cities

Globalisation - sometimes defined as a "generalisation of cultures" - is evident everywhere, China, Africa, South America are all influenced by radically different Western cultures and, in a different way, we are influenced by them. Globalisation has not occurred in the way predicted. We are not one world, one people; and cultures have not completely blended or become homogenised. The French and English are not now more like each other, in fact the reverse could be argued (Mommaas 1997).

Globalisation via media and communications has created an increasingly crowded market place, and one of the effects is the need to differentiate yourself, your individuality and your place.

The interesting, ironic twist is that in an effort to distinguish say England, Scotland and Wales, there has been a tendency to fall back on antiquarian, slightly nationalistic, two dimensional, stereotypical interpretations of these richly layered identities. Variety has been rejected in favour of the easily digestible and simplistic.

'Celtic Wales', 'Royal England' (in reality the 'Home Counties') and 'The Scotland of William Wallace' (*Braveheart* was in fact filmed mainly in Ireland by Americans and starred an Australian) may be easy advertising buy-lines, but it is not clear what they really mean and where they leave culturally diverse sections of and personalities within the population that typically make up our cities. This includes minority ethnic communities from Asia and Africa, but also from Europe, including Italy, Ireland, Poland and elsewhere, young people, old people, disabled people and others.

This is what distinguishes place from place, city from city. The innovative interpretation of identity, the promotion of local cultural features and the way complex and challenging issues have been dealt with creatively expresses the personality and individuality of places.

Globalisation increases choice: of holiday; of business location; of habitat. Cities are no longer competing in the same region or country, but on a global level, which has led to the growth of place marketing world-wide. It has resulted in the need for the development industry to be more creative as property cannot meet market demands if developed out of context with its locality. The essential point is that locations cannot seek to be competitive by following a purely economic agenda as added value is also created by incorporating the cultural texture and values of a place.

For the 21st Century city, to be competitive means standing apart from the crowd. Even though information and communication technology has given many companies the freedom to locate almost anywhere, they still gravitate towards cities.

"Cities provide an ideal platform for innovation, a balanced infrastructure, people, information and access to contracted out functions and a subtle mix of attributes. Cities also provide clout, weight and kudos to companies. These can be subjective and difficult to define, but are real factors in the company relocation process." (Lewis)

Brindley Place, Birmingham

Brindley Place is a commercial development in the heart of an old industrial district in Birmingham. The project was led by Argent PLC, a commercial developer. Instead of taking a short-term approach, cutting corners on specification and design quality, the developer has considered carefully that factors that will provide a long-term return on their investment. This has resulted in a new commercial quarter for Birmingham, which promises to be a sustainable environment for the future. The development has integrated many features that relate to the heritage of the area, creating a sense of real identity and distinctiveness. It has also considered carefully quality of life factors and the quality of the urban space and public realm, investing heavily in individual building design, public space and cultural and leisure facilities. This distinctiveness gives Brindley Place a competitive edge, convincing a traditional occupier market to relocate to a former industrial zone.

As a footnote to this example, Argent PLC have recently decided to reconsider their leasing arrangements, particularly in relation to large chains. They have realised that bringing in local independent traders greatly increases the local flavour of the development. This may result in an initial loss from the retail rentals, but Argent have realised that any minor loss at ground level will be more than compensated for by the increased success of renting office space as a result of such a unique local offer.

Exploring and reflecting local identity through community participation in order to create sense of place can result in significant competitive advantages for individual buildings, towns, cities and regions. This advantage helps to secure tenants, buyers and business relocations and retention, assuring the commercial success of development schemes.

There is, thus, a direct, tangible and traceable link between good place marketing practice, positive place identity, community participation and commercial property and land values.

Three fundamental problems

The research has identified three fundamental problems with place marketing practice:.

1. Content

The content of the messages are largely: uninteresting; unrepresentative; backward looking; and do not seem to work very well. The content of campaigns needs to be revisited in a radical and innovative way, conveying powerful new messages about new relationships. These messages need to consider iconic communication, getting complex messages across simply. The messages need to be finessed and nuanced conveying a deeper sense of reality and authenticity about the place.

2. Process

Place marketing practice is rooted in product marketing. Some tools and ideas are transferable, but the reductive approach has little relevance to the complexities of place. A new set of models, tools and approaches which are up to the demands of the job need to be developed to meet the specific challenges of sophisticated place marketing. In doing this we need to involve local players, turning residents into Ambassadors and tapping in to their knowledge and creativity.

3. Integration

There is a lack of integration between place marketing and place development - place marketing is often an add-on to all the other activity in a place. It selectively promotes what exits rather than being a constant thread in the planning, development and policy making for the area. Place marketing could offer much to help develop the environment it attempts to promote.

Above all, practice needs to develop a more authentic and honest approach. Honest marketing messages can be enormously powerful, simply because people recognise hype when they see it, distrust it and in the end see through it and are disappointed. They also recognise honesty and are touched by it in a different way. It is ironic that the Advertising Code of Conduct requires that messages are "decent, legal, honest and truthful", yet few of us would really trust advertising in this way.

An alternative, Cultural Planning approach

Recently, definitions of culture have begun to shift. The Department for Culture Media and Sport (DCMS) has by its very existence broadened the definition from a euphemism for 'arts', to include a range of other activities, like the creative industries (1998), including businesses which have creativity at their core. This policy thrust has been supported by other initiatives that have moved the cultural sector from the policy margins to a position where its contribution to education and social inclusion can no longer be doubted (see the strategy reports: *All our Futures*, NACCCE and DfEE – now DfES - (1999), *Arts and Sports*, PAT 10, DCMS (1999)).

Cultural planning takes the contribution of culture to another level. It broadens the definition to include way of life factors, highlighting anything that fundamentally influences or contributes to the quality of life of a place, which it sees as being defined by a recognition of the cultures of its inhabitants. This is a culturally-focused approach to the development of policy and planning in areas that are largely viewed as non-cultural, particularly those concerned with the built environment and infrastructure.

In so doing it attempts to identify and harness local creativity and cultural understanding to any given challenge of urban policy and planning. In this way, new, innovative and previously unthought of solutions and connections can be made to solve old and apparently intractable challenges of urban living. As Franco Bianchini has pointed out (1999 p87) a culturally aligned perspective tends to be:

"a) holistic, interdisciplinary, intercultural and lateral;
b) innovation-oriented, original and experimental;
c) critical, inquiring, challenging and questioning;
d) people-centred, humanistic, and non-deterministic;
e) 'cultured' and informed by critical knowledge of traditions of cultural expression."

These key elements are then reproduced and incorporated in the planning and policy development processes. They are precisely the elements that are lacking in the research literature, which by contrast is largely:

- monocultural and stereotypical;
- lacking in innovation, unoriginal and undistinctive;
- not at all inquiring or challenging of stereotypes;
- imposed without consultation; and
- regards culture as homogeneous, rooted in the past, not the present.

A more inclusive, innovative and ultimately successful model of place marketing in the UK that applies this perspective would allow place marketing to evolve as a central tool in the regeneration, renewal and overall development of 'places'. Without corrective action, the flawed practice uncovered in the research will continue to alienate, disenfranchise and, ultimately, to fail.

The future of place marketing practice - six key actions

1. Integration

A more integrated form of multi-disciplinary practice should be developed, drawing from a wide range of professional and academic disciplines which links to place development, regeneration and renewal. There should be more coordination between public and private sectors in thinking through place marketing jointly whose boundaries are increasingly blurring in any case.

Their aims are different, but the commercial sector shares a growing realisation of the benefits of long term investments in a place, that are secured through strong relationships with residents and their identities. In some cases, a commercial personality is very closely woven into a place's character, particularly when a large employer is based there, such as Pilkingtons in St. Helens. This can be a fragile balance, and the last recession is full of examples of it faltering, particularly where mining or textiles were involved.

Yet the more integrated approach is likely to have more chance of success in these circumstances, and the Huddersfield Creative Town Initiative is a useful example. Its cross-cutting approach helped to unearth and to mobilise - literally to begin to 'mine' - a new kind of wealth in the city; the local cultural resources, the talent and creativity of its local people.

It implies private and public sector marketing professionals taking on board and involving more divergent views including those of: artists; sociologists; psychologists; health professionals; the justice system; environmentalists; urban geographers; planners; architects; community representatives and others. These multi-disciplinary teams can conduct the business of analysing, improving and promoting the place in a more coherent and integrated way.

By so doing it ensures that any project operates across sectors and local government departments, with an injection of new ideas and perspectives. This in turn will generate more imaginative and creative approaches to place marketing, based on an area's distinctiveness, its past, the whole of its present and importantly, its aspirations for the future.

2. Participate to innovate

Innovation will develop as a natural consequence of the integrated approach, but also needs to evolve from participatory projects. Innovation begins with an idea, but is developed through real projects.

Consultation is important, but deeper participation can yield far richer results. Consultation is often, mistakenly, seen as a consensus-building process. Participation extends this process creating a two-way flow of information, engaging people with the issues. At the same time it builds capacity not just to grasp the issues - which most people usually do -

but to raise expectations and aspirations about what might be possible, how things might be different. To do this effectively people need to be given the tools to participate - a seat at the table on its own is of little use.

'Planning for Real' and the recent Place-Check initiative, specifically aimed at involving children in urban planning, are examples of how a kind of ideas bank can be created; which Bianchini and Schwengel (1991) describe as "a resource bank of ideas, images, experiences and perspectives relating to that locality". Cowan's Place-Check engages young people with a specific set of issues and tasks, researching the urban environment and thinking about its development.

Some ideas may be useful now, some tomorrow, but the central point is that the ideas can come from anywhere, and professionals do not have a monopoly on good ideas. Thereby local cultural resources are mobilised, unlocking creativity, and using it to develop and move forward, turning local residents into local ambassadors.

To gain confidence in the new approach a series of local pilot projects should be initiated. The projects would produce real results in themselves, but also lead to a new way of interpreting and promoting places.

Place-Check involves young people in urban development and they are every bit as important in place marketing and we need to find ways to involve them. Purely in terms of tourism, they represent a major market segment. Around 25 million visits annually to the UK are made by under 25s, spending a collective £2.4 billion. They tend to be market innovators and blaze a trail to new kinds of tourist destinations. Evidence suggests (Beaton, L. 1999, p10) that they are interested in diversity, difference and distinctiveness, as well as heritage and the arts.

This is the future - what they are interested in now the majority will be tomorrow. They are market innovators, blazing a trail to new destinations as we speak, but there is no evidence of them in the research literature.

3. From place marketing to place development

There is a wider role for place marketing given its potential to become a tool for urban and community development and conflict resolution. Yet, taking a critical, questioning and honest role is a difficult path for traditional marketing to follow as it tends to embellish and only highlight the positive. It would be like exposing a product flaw in advertising, 'this is the vacuum that nearly cleans up to the edge'. It may seem unlikely, but the conflict of the past and present can, if handled creatively, lead to innovative marketing solutions, as in South Africa.

South Africa - turning conflict into discovery

Acknowledging conflict and division is essential in finding a real solution in any situation. A strategic meeting held in autumn 2000 attended by the country's leading practitioners and government officials in South Africa discussed its branding as a tourist destination. The meeting began by sifting through some old-style marketing messages used by other countries. Sand was rejected as a core brand because Egypt had cornered the market on sand, Kenya had got lions and elephants, the Gold Coast had sea, so what were they going to do? What was it that was different about South Africa?

Stepping back from these core brands, the group was encouraged to take a more culturally focused look at the identity of South Africa, what it was and what it represented. They realised that South Africa's history of conflict was perhaps its best known feature; something as difficult to celebrate as it is to deny. Exploring this further, the group discussed the new, emerging identity of the country, as a journey of self discovery on which it has embarked after decades of struggle. The idea was that this journey of self discovery could be reflected in tourism, inviting the visitor to take part in their own journey of self-discovery. In a sense, this allows the visitor to create their own experience, their own tailor made product from an infinite menu of choices. It also created a great opportunity for a distinctive campaign.

This approach could be adopted at a more local level. Linking place marketing to regeneration schemes and community development programmes could provide benefits in two directions. The schemes and programmes would benefit from this more authentic and honest approach to promoting their activities and place marketers would be given a vast new range of content to include in their campaigns.

Netherfield - marketing and regeneration working together

Netherfield is a housing estate within a regeneration area in Milton Keynes. Built as an early part of the new town, it has experienced significant challenges. The regeneration partnership has funded a wide variety of cultural projects from public art programmes to sports and arts events.

The Partnership also funded the creation of a small marketing agency to carry out evaluation and research on its behalf. The agency is composed of local residents who have received training through the regeneration scheme. As well as monitoring the results of the regeneration initiative, the agency has carried out local need audits, to enable precise targeting of resources for future projects and how they should be marketed. The agency became a central feature of the regeneration scheme, funded through the Single Regeneration Budget. It demonstrated that market has an inward, local and developmental role as well as an outwardly focused promotional one. Gathering information, testing assumptions and building networks to aid place development were as important as any external marketing of the scheme.

It does not require a leap of imagination to see how useful a broader agency like Netherfield could be, combining place development with place marketing. Bringing together top down and bottom up approaches yields more effective results as top down on its own is likely to continue to alienate and disenfranchise, resulting in the literature researched. Repositioning elements of place marketing away from the centre may help, giving people the tools to communicate their own particular perspective on the place. Community and internet radio and alternative newspapers are examples that can help to achieve this, and can be self financing, adding a great deal to the area, for instance *Hip Hop fm* in New York and *Radio Multikulti* in Berlin. *Hip hop fm* is funded by a software developer, keen to see how the station can experiment with new technology. *Radio Multikulti* is an energetic, open access multicultural radio station, allowing people a voice, not just to communicate their exclusion, but to celebrate their own cultures. These initiatives do much more than simply market a 'place'; they provide a platform for engagement and empowerment of otherwise marginal groups, they add to the flavour and texture of a place, they get that place known and they provide content for wider promotional campaigns.

The Bristol Style

A sub-section in *Bristol city and countryside* goes into some detail about local popular culture. Realising the potential for 'youth-tourism' and the distinctiveness that a lively popular culture can give to a city, they have given this some profile in their publicity.

The bands and performers Portishead, Massive Attack, Roni Size and Tricky are all mentioned, alongside the existing 24 hour club culture. The profile is quite small within the brochure, but is in sharp contrast to many others, where nothing appears to have happened in the area for 500 years. Alternative, popular and minority cultures are part of 'places' identity. Recognising this is not only important in including those communities; it can create a real difference for visitors faced with multiple choices and a stronger position in the tourism market.

New tools need developing to shift practice into the field of place development and the toolkit suggested below, including the Place Development Matrix represents a start.

4. The right tools for the job: a new place marketers toolkit

Comedia has developed a cultural planning toolkit, as outlined in *The Creative City* (Landry, 2000). It includes techniques – even tricks - that force a shift in perception. Looking at an issue from a child's perspective, for example, or renaming 'housing' as 'habitat', or 'transport' as 'communication and access' in a local authority are examples used to show how a simple shift can broaden perspectives and disclose new opportunities and creative solutions.

Place marketing needs a similar bag of tools to bring to bear on its own practice and in the way it develops plans and strategies.

Landry talks about turning the planning process on its head, about "imagining forwards and planning backwards" (2000) and this is what place marketing needs to do. We have to imagine a vision for the future of place marketing practice as a whole and for individual projects and campaigns, and then plan backwards to put in place the steps that will take us there.

Local audits of more than just facilities, taking in cultural factors, sights, sounds and smells, different elements of personality and the whole feel, taste and texture of a place are needed to generate new material and new content for place marketing messages.

I am not necessarily suggesting 'scratch and sniff' brochures, but actually, perhaps I am. Brochures could be more interactive, particularly their electronic counterparts on the web, which are, with some exceptions, just electronic versions of the same thing. Pop-ups, music, recordings like the ones found in greetings cards, quizzes, games, activities for adults as well as children, things that at once involve you in the act of discovery and investigation, and in the place.

URBANIS - exploring the past, creating the future

URBANIS is an international multimedia heritage project. Led by my unit at Milton Keynes Council, it involved partners in museums in Rome and Mainz, Germany and was funded by the European Commission.

Each partner made an interactive CD, which collectively told the story of how the ideas behind their towns and cities began in Europe, which were transformed by the Romans and as they spread across the continent.

The Milton Keynes CD was produced by the BBC Multimedia Unit based at the Open University in Milton Keynes. It is completely interactive, aimed at older children but of interest to adults. It is based on a series of maps that show activity and settlement through the ages in Milton Keynes, from dinosaurs to the present day. Children can click on a particular area to reveal archaeological finds near to their school, house or estate.

The artefacts are not displayed just as photographs though; the CD includes video, re-enactments, animations, games and interactive quizzes and challenges the user to understand how ideas about how we live evolved and why. Having grasped some sense of urban development through the ages, users then enter the URBANIS *Game Zone*. Here they can build their own interactive city, which lives and breathes and responds to the way it is built. This can be seen from a set of changing indicators about crime, the economy, employment, housing repair and so on.

URBANIS brings the past to life, but in so doing it gives people a stake in their future, makes them think about what it might be like and have a go at developing their own version of this. More than anything, URBANIS reveals and exposes the processes of urban living and involves the user in them.

The process for doing this need not be dry, but could be managed through a project in which people participate, involving the Higher Education sector in developing new research methods and teasing out just what the results mean. This may bring to light undisclosed or hidden cultural assets and local features which might be used in campaigns. It will also help to generate new and more ideas, which can be used to set objectives.

The objectives of some of the brochures were unclear, perhaps an attempt to promote the area generally, to generate business for hotels or to generate wider tourism, or even a mix of these. But other objectives might also have been included, such as describing the rich texture of their areas, so reflecting its present as well as its past, thereby giving people a real flavour of the area's potential and creating a feeling of inclusion, sense of place, ownership and pride amongst local people so moving on from stereotypes.

Having set itself objectives, place marketing needs to know when it has worked, how well it has worked and have some indication of why. Not just statistically - evaluation models need to be radically revisited, working up new sets of qualitative indicators. It is complex, but not impossible as Francois Matarrasso (1997) and others have shown. It is not necessary to provide evidence that goes beyond reasonable doubt. Marketing has a scientific, statistical component, but at the end of the day is based on judgement calls, famously expressed in the saying that "most companies know half their advertising budget is wasted, they just don't know which half".

Traditional marketing tools might also be adapted. The Product Life Cycle coupled with something like Ansoff's Matrix (two marketing tools used to analyse competitive position and plan strategies for the future (Lancaster and Massingham 1993)), might provide some useful clues about place marketing strategies, but should be used very judiciously. The General Electric Portfolio Matrix, a business and marketing planning tool, has been usefully adapted to other fields, such as fundraising, and might be so for place marketing, as a matrix for planning broader place development initiatives.

The Place Development Matrix

The General Electric Portfolio Matrix (Lancaster and Massingham 1993) is a standard in the product marketer's toolkit. It is a tried and tested planning grid to enable decisions on which market or business segments should be developed and which should be stabilised or wound down. It assesses two linked factors, market attractiveness and competitive position, ranking them high, medium or low. The matrix then suggests strategies. For example, if a business or product has a strong competitive position (a market leader) but the market is only averagely attractive (perhaps saturated with similar products), the matrix suggests: investing in more attractive segments; building ability to take on opposition; or raising productivity as a profit strategy.

Turning this on its head, we can examine what the two linked factors would be for place development, connected to place marketing. The level of local aspirations and capacity within the community – thinking ahead to a better future and having the motivation and skills to get there - might replace 'market attractiveness'. 'Competitive position' might be replaced by 'local resources', not just money, but facilities, access to lifelong learning, advice and information and other support from local agencies.

Plotting these factors on a matrix gives a sense of where and how to target resources in regeneration and renewal schemes, including the intervention of a new kind of place marketing agency.

On the Matrix shown below, 'Reconsider investment' might relate to a project which has been successful in raising money, but not targeted the real issues. 'Sustain development' is a successful scheme that may become self-sustaining. At each point on the Matrix, there is a role for reconceived place marketing, in: building capacity; developing sense of place; revealing local identity; and generating new aspirations.

The Place Development Matrix

Local aspirations

HIGH	***Sustain development*** Free-up resources for use elsewhere and roll-out as a model of good practice.	***Build local capacity*** Mobilise high local aspirations to increase level of resources through own efforts.	***Invest in aspiration*** Aspirations high but resource needed to move locality to *Build local capacity* stage.
MEDIUM	***Refocus resources*** Review use of resources to shift the locality to *Sustain development* position. Some resources may no longer be needed.	***Build resources and capacity*** Available resources equal local aspirations; increase both by mobilising the community.	***Invest in capacity*** Resources needed to develop capacity and aspirations, which still exist despite low investment.
LOW	***Reconsider investment*** A high level of resources is not building aspirations and should be refocused or reconsidered.	***Continue investment*** A sustained and focused investment needed to raise aspiration levels.	***Increase investment*** Little history of investment and few aspirations. Resource – injection needed to get the ball rolling.
	HIGH	**MEDIUM**	**LOW**

Local resources

Although adapting existing tools is possible and useful, it is insufficient. Place marketing needs to develop its own set of innovative and radical analytical tools that take account of a range of qualitative factors currently unaccounted for in the more quantitative approach of traditional marketing.

Practically, such tools will need to be created through research, involving other sectors, particularly Higher Education, and will need to be tested. Imagery and descriptive text are essential items in the place marketer's arsenal. Expertise in these areas is not confined to, or even led by, the marketing field. Artists, writers and other kinds of cultural producers can help us to see places and the way they are represented in new and different ways. Examples include new environments like Bluewater, and the housing estate that now covers Midlesborough's old football ground, Ayresome Park, which has subtle traces of the past poking through into the present; a public art scheme that includes corner flags, bronze footballs and penalty spots. La Sala Borsa in Bologna develops this approach.

La Sala Borsa

Bologna's Borsa is a re-conceived library that combines the local past present and future in a unique way, with elegant simplicity. Whilst renovating a 19th Century stock exchange as part of the new library development in the centre of Bologna, workers discovered a Roman street underneath. Whilst this should come as no surprise when digging in Italy, what was unusual was the discovery of a two thousand year old basilica beneath the stock exchange. The basilica was the centre of the local and regional economy in Roman times, a place where merchants met to strike deals.

In the same way that the basilica was the centre for the exchange of goods, the stock exchange, built in ignorance above it, became the centre for the symbolic exchange of goods through stocks and shares. The new Borsa is now the scene of a constant exchange of massive amounts of information, something that is as important now for the local and regional economy as the stock exchange and basilica where in their day. To express this link through time, part of the library's floor is glass, exposing the Roman street and basilica beneath to view. As well as the self contained eloquence of the project, it builds on Bologna's traditions and heritage as a centre of literature and publishing, connecting a wide range of communities of interest.

One of the tools in this kit should the ability to work effectively with local communities in developing place marketing strategies, avoiding at all costs the so called 'smile campaigns'.

"By focusing on a destination-community's heritage and culture in the development of its tourism product, the industry will not only present a truer picture of the destination, it will become an ally of many public interest groups."

(Murphy, 1991, p151).

This is essential to avoid destructive stereotyping which, in the extreme, has led to confusions such as members of the Cherokee tribe in the Great Smoky Mountains National Park, Northern America, being constantly portrayed as wearing war bonnets and living in tepees - something that was never part of their culture.

Heritage is an important tool and, as the research has identified, the one most commonly used. It is not just about a glorified dim and distant past, but one that reveals its tensions as well, taps into the recent past and the living present. This idea is typified by the Ecomusee movement in France, championed by Hugue de Varinne.

***Ecomusee* - living local heritage**

The Ecomusee movement began in France as a collaboration between communities, museums professionals and artists. It was championed by Hugue de Varinne, Secretary General of the International Council of Museums. Ecomusee are often extremely small - sometimes just one room - and are not collection-focused museums, where preservation of the archive is everything and visitors are sometimes seen as a necessary evil.

Ecomusee have defined geographical territories, which can be quite small. They are about specific local heritage. They take a multidisciplinary approach, are not built just on archaeology and believe that oral history is as important as artefacts. These 'musee' also see education and interpretation as their primary function, not as an add-on to a preservation-oriented strategy.

The projects see the whole of the community as their 'customer', not just regular visitors, and they give control of policy and activity programmes to representatives of that community.

This approach creates a vast archive of images, ideas, experiences and artefacts. This rich cultural resource can then be used as an effective place marketing tool, engaging local communities with their own heritage whilst promoting it to others.

Visual and other art forms provide another potential tool. Contemporary art has been used very effectively to interpret the past whilst promoting the present. Anthony Gormley's *Angel of the North*, situated by the A1 on the approach to Newcastle, is perhaps the best known example in the UK. A colossal iconic monument it celebrates the industrial heritage of the area and provides a message about its present and its future. It has been so well accepted as a symbol of the area that it now appears on almost every local tourism publication, challenging - or perhaps complementing - the marketing of 'Catherine Cookson Country'.

Used alongside more traditional heritage, contemporary art can expose the links, contrasts and connections between past and present, revealing places as living habitats, rather than pickled, like 'Brigadoons', preserved at a perfect moment in a fictional past.

Above all, place marketing needs to get creative and stay creative. To do this, it needs to radically reshape its thinking and the tools it uses, finding news ways to innovate and explore what places really mean. Training and continuing professional development packages will kick-start this process.

5. Breaking the mould - retraining the professionals

Place marketing is a growing discipline and practice. Currently, there is little professional training available to people working in this field who wish to go beyond more general or product oriented marketing. This is a major problem, as practice needs to develop and the tendency towards reductive solutions be resisted.

We have seen alternative marketing training for service sector professionals and, more recently, for the arts sector. This latter course was developed jointly by the Arts Marketing Association and the Chartered Institute for Marketing. For place marketing, this training might include the wider picture described above, connecting place marketing with place development.

Training of this kind also brings a wide mix of professionals together, to share ideas, experience and best practice. To develop comprehensive new professional standards in this emerging discipline, it may be worth creating a professional body, ideally pan-European. This body might develop and validate learning packages, create a membership and continuing professional development scheme and regulate practice, providing a code of ethical practice and conduct for its members. The creation of such a body would help to create, maintain and develop new standards of professional practice in place marketing.

An embryo exists in the UK's Culture and Tourism Group, consisting of the Arts Council's of England Scotland and Wales, Tourist Boards and RESOURCE, the libraries, museums, archives and galleries national body.

The creation of a European award for best place marketing practice would additionally help in progressing this agenda. However, as discussed earlier, for this to happen, for the training to be effective and to create the fundamental shift in practice that is needed, new theoretical models and practical marketing tools need to be developed – and existing ones adapted, to meet the particular, peculiar and demanding nature of place marketing. This includes constantly challenging our ideas and perceptions about a place, championing authenticity and innovative representation.

6. Shifting the mind-set: a new definition of place

The history and identity of a place is shaped entirely by human action and perception, through time. This is of course influenced by landscape, seascape, climate and other geographical features, but what we are really seeing when we look at a place is the result of human intervention and narrative. What Roijakkers (1999) called a mindscape rather than a landscape.

Much current practice appears to randomly bag a limited set of facts about the heritage, geography and imagined culture of a place. It thus lacks authenticity and depth and in consequence is less effective. Rooijakkers (1999) reminds us that identity is about perception, not things.

"Identity is never monolithic, and it never exists outside man. It is not attached to soil and locations; the locations are appropriated in a cultural way by people; thus the landscape becomes a 'mindscape'."

The identity of the place *is* about the people who live there. So one must ask how a place marketing programme can connect with local identity if they are not included. The complexity, difficulty and diversity of the present should be seen as a rich palette from which to draw, rather than being glossed over, hiding it behind a selective view of the past.

This allows us to move away from the stereotypes and clichés uncovered in the research and to explore alternative models, to re-examine the relationship between past and present as in the *Borse* example.

Places are not static, but constantly changing and shifting. This makes life difficult but more interesting for the place marketer. It requires the marketer to constantly redefine 'place' in relation to their own territory, but it allows us to substitute bland stereotypes for richness and diversity in our publications.

Authenticity and layers of different representations and perceptions of 'place' allow people to create their own 'product', their own experience, from an infinite menu of choices. The visitor and resident alike can then embark on new journeys and unearth unique experiences, adding to the identity and meaning of that place as they do so.

Summary and conclusions

Places are cultural entities. People gather to work, live, build cities, to play. Their activity generates a way of life, a culture, which it would be wrong to see as an incidental by-product of human activity. On the contrary, it is the central feature and reason for gathering in the first instance.

Local identity, distinctiveness, sense of place and creativity are as essential to local economic renewal and vitality now as an available workforce and some natural mineral resources were one hundred years ago. At the threshold of the information age, creativity is what makes that information useful; without it, the information is a worthless mass.

Regarding places as living cultural entities rather than inanimate machines, the localised culture and the creativity they contain become a fantastic resource. This resource can be mobilised and used to regenerate or expand the local economy, as many European examples show. It can also be used as the cornerstone of a re-visioned kind of place marketing practice.

This means we have to think again and see places in all their complex wonderfulness accepting and work with it. This inquiry into place marketing reveals the following key issues.

Seven central issues

1.

Place marketing literature represents places as bland, homogenous and simple, disregarding many of the more interesting facets of local culture and ignoring difficult local complexities. Instead of messages imbued with the psyche of the area, a sham historical pageant is paraded through the brochure's pages.

2.

Literature of this kind has not been proven to work very effectively. Where research evidence is available, it is not encouraging. Further research into the quantitative and qualitative impacts of place marketing needs putting in place.

3.

Places, cities and regions are best regarded as living, evolving, cultural entities with an existence of their own, not as theme parks for visitors. This recognition allows important local cultural resources, ingenuity and creativity to be mobilised, bringing a sense of distinctiveness and in its wake, economic success and more visitors. The commercial sector's awareness of the importance of character and distinctiveness in competitive success is growing fast and may leave the public sector behind.

4.

Marketing places as cultural entities will involve rethinking the content of messages and carefully examining the tools and processes which are used to develop and then communicate these messages. Developing 'iconic communication' is essential. Messages must move from the burlesque to the authentic, resonating with the reality of local experience. A research agenda undertaken with partners in other fields needs to be developed to achieve this.

5.

This involves rethinking and redefining what we mean by terms and ideas such as 'place', 'landscape', even 'history', and recognising fully the importance of human action and perception in shaping these.

6.

Place marketing efforts reflect the social relations of a locality and these relations, particularly between dominant and excluded groups, need to change as part of comprehensive and sustainably successful place marketing campaigns. This makes the shift from place marketing to place development.

7.

An agenda for action, based on the six point plan highlighted needs to be evolved to fundamentally shift place marketing practice from its current position, if it is to have a central role in the future promotion and development of, cities and regions.

The vast weighting in the literature in favour of the past over the present is troubling. The use of often fictitious or partial heritage is a short term, unsustainable tactic. It parodies the past and disrespects the present, excluding, denying other heritages and implying a call to return to a more hierarchical 'Golden Age' and results in regimented and monosyllabic promotional content. A shift in place marketing practice means a shift away from these representations and in community relationships. It will be necessary to bring people in from the margins, to reflect local diversity and address issues of social inclusion positively, to make place marketing campaigns a touchstone of the real.

Inventive messages imbued with local flavour will ultimately become a sustainable and integrated element of an overall local development strategy, in which place marketing has the opportunity to take centre stage. Pilot projects are necessary to carry forward these ideas and some indications of change can be seen in the UK and elsewhere.

There is a final and saddening footnote to this text. Following the terrorist attacks of September 11th in New York, tourism authorities predict a recession for the industry with 900,000 job losses word wide. If international tourism declines, it is all the more necessary to put in place an action plan to revitalise our place marketing and ensure we connect with local audiences.

To realise its potential, a sea-change is needed that will reposition place marketing as a practice that is: creative, truly local; participatory and inclusive; innovative and un-stereotypical; multidisciplinary; and not based on product marketing. The action points above make some suggestions about how this work could begin. What is essential is action. As Eric Reynolds of Urban Space Management said (1999):

"Goethe had a lovely phrase, "whatever you want to do, or dream you could do, begin it." Starting has magic in it. Sitting about on your hands doesn't."

Bibliography

Adams, E. and Ingham, S. (1998): *Changing Places, children's participation in environmental planning;* The Children's Society, London.

Beaton, L. (1999) in; Hill, L. (ed); *c&t, the newsletter of the UK Culture and Tourism Group*; issue 2, Dec 1999.

Bianchini, F. (1999): *The relationship between cultural resources and tourism policies for cities and regions*; in; Dodd, D. & van Hemel, A. (eds): *Planning Cultural Tourism in Europe;* Boekman Foundation, Amsterdam; pp 78-90.

Creative Industries Task Force (1998): *Creative Industries Mapping Document*; DCMS, London.

Erickson, B. and Roberts, M. (1997): *Marketing local identity*; in: *Journal of Urban Design*, Vol 1, No. 2. pp 35-59.

Forrester in, Kotler, P (1991): *Marketing Management, Analysis, Planning, Implementation and Control*; Prentice Hall inc.; America,.

Krippendorf, K. (1980): *Content Analysis, an Introduction to its Methodology*; Sage, Newbury Park, CA.

Kotler, P. (1993): *Marketing Places - Attracting Investment, Industry and Tourism to Cities, States and Nations*; The Free Press, NY.

Lancaster, G. and Massingham, L. (1993): *Essentials of Marketing, Second Edition*; McGraw Hill Book Company Europe, Maidenhead.

Landry, C. (2000):*The Creative City: a toolkit for urban innovators*; Earthscan Publications Ltd (for COMEDIA), London.

Matarrasso, F. (1997) *Use or Ornament - the social impact of participation in the arts*; Comedia, Bournes Green.

Mommaas, H. (1997): *Globalisation and cultural policies; implications for European cities*; presentation notes for MA European Cultural Planning.

Murphy, P.E. (1991): *Tourism, a Community Approach*; Routledge, London.

NACCCE (National Advisory Committee on Creative and Cultural Education) (1999); *All Our Futures*; DfEE, London.

Pachter, M and Landry, C (2001): Culture at the Crossroads: Culture and Cultural Institutions at the beginning of the 21st Century; COMEDIA, Bournes Green.

Policy Action Team 10. (1999) *Arts and Sports*; DCMS.

Reynolds, E. (1999): in; Milton Keynes Council (eds): *Cultural Planning Bulletin - Cultural planning seminar at De Montfort University*; Milton Keynes Council.

Rooijakkers, G. (1999): *Identity Factory Southeast; Towards a Flexible Cultural Leisure Infrastructure;* in, Dodd, D. and van Hemel, A. (eds) *Planning Cultural Tourism in Europe;* Boekman Foundation, Amsterdam; pp 101-111.

Thomas, N. & Adams, M. (1999).*Cook's Sites: revisiting history;*University of Otago Press; Dunedin, NZ.

Worpole, K. and Greenhalgh, L. (1999): *The Richness of Cities, urban policy in a new landscape, Final Report*; Comedia/DEMOS, London.

Recent Comedia publications

Culture at the Crossroads: Culture and cultural institutions at the beginning of the 21st century

'Culture at the crossroads re-imagines the 21st century cultural landscape. For the perplexed it is the book we have been looking for.

^The discussions on which 'Culture at the Crossroads' is based were one of the most stimulating occasions I have experienced, provoking deep thought about how culture has changed in the last half century and how cultural institutions have — and should — be responding to such changes'. Charles Saumarez Smith, director of the National Portrait Gallery, London

Marc Pachter & Charles Landry, 110 pages, A5, £9.00

The Creative City: A toolkit for urban innovators

Draws on examples from around the world to set out a new radical vision for cities, with creative solutions to their problems. '*The Creative City will be one of the key urban texts of the next decade. It is a truly millennial book and shows how new modes of thinking can help regenerate cities facing the challenge of survival.'*- Sir Peter Hall, Bartlett Professor of Planning, University College, London.

Charles Landry, 300 pages A5 £17.95

Resourcing Culture: Briefing Papers on Culture and Development

Culture is increasingly recognised as crucial to sustainable human development because it is our cultural values which determine our goals and sense of fulfilment. Development processes which fail to recognise and which simplistically divide peoples resources from their aspirations or their health from how they feel struggle to produce lasting improvements. If we are to meet the challenges of the new century we will have to engage with development in the context and through the medium of human cultures.

Edited by Francois Matarasso Contributors include: Carol Steinberg, Helen Gould, Kit Grauer, Yohanna Loucheur, Danielle Cliché, Nestor Garcia Canclini. 96 pages A4 £10 2001

The Richness of Cities

The final report of this acclaimed new study (with 12 associated working papers) signals a radical new way of thinking about urban policy. It celebrates the power of modern cities to act a crucibles of innovative solutions to the great economic, social and environmental issues of our time. **Final Report Liz Greenhalgh & Ken Worpole, 72 pages A4 £15 1999**

Use or Ornament? The Social Impact of Participation in the Arts

This major report looks at the impact of participation in arts activities at local level, drawing on dozens of projects from the Western Isles to Portsmouth, and beyond the UK. The report reveals the vital role they play in the life of communities of all kinds contributing directly to their skills base, long-term confidence and viability. It argues for recognition of their value by Government, local authorities and other bodies concerned with social development. It also argues that the publicly-funded arts world should take greater account of its social responsibilities, and seek to work actively with social policy partners.

François Matarasso 120 pp. A4 £20 1997

Innovative and Sustainable Cities

An assessment survey and evaluation of over 500 urban innovations and best practices from over 20 countries in Europe, covering environmental, social, business and cultural initiatives to complete a six year study by the European Foundation for Living and Working Conditions. Includes a taxonomy of urban innovations.

Sir Peter Hall & Charles Landry, 113 pages A4 £15 1998

Learning development

Draws on new research into the impact of libraries on personal and community development in the context of current issues such as education and learning, employment, families and young people, poverty, health, social inclusion, local democracy and culture. The report is a short and readable introduction. While library professionals will find it a useful pointer to new research, it will help elected members, professionals in other services and students to gain a broader understanding of public libraries.

François Matarasso, 72 pages A5 £6, 1998

Beyond book issues: the social potential of library projects

Reviews projects submitted to the Holt Jackson/Library Association Community Initiative awards to assess the extent to which these projects produce social benefits. It finds substantial outcomes for personal and community development, concluding that library projects and outreach work have a valuable role to play in community growth. The study concludes that the existing library performance indicators are an inadequate management tool for the library of the 21st century, given its educational, leisure and community development functions.

François Matarasso, 60 pages A4 £15, 1998

Parklife: urban parks and social renewal

Recently described as 'a report which will change forever our perception of urban parks and open spaces within our towns and cities', Park Life covers every conceivable aspect of the crisis facing the funding, management, and use of open space in Britain's towns and cities. Details of the 12 park working papers published in 1996 are available on request.

Liz Greenhalgh & Ken Worpole, £20 1997

All publications available through:

Eco-Distribution
Crosswell,
Eglywswrw,
Pembrokeshire,
SA41 3TE
0123 989 1431
jill.chandler@virgin.netCulture